CRM Mastery

The Sales Ops Manager's Guide to
Elevating Customer Relationships and Sales
Performance

Jeff Nguyen

Contents

Introduction to CRM in Sales Ops

C ustomer relationship management (CRM) software has become a vital component of running a successful modern business. By centralizing customer data and interactions across an organization, CRM empowers companies to provide personalized, timely service that breeds loyalty.

This guide explores the origins of CRM technology, its continuous evolution over the past several decades, and expected future advancements. We will learn how early digital contact management systems laid the groundwork for today's multifaceted platforms. We will also examine how emerging capabilities like artificial intelligence and machine learning are reshaping CRMs.

Understanding this history provides critical context for business leaders and sales operations teams seeking to optimize their customer engagement strategy and supporting technologies. When we comprehend how far CRM has come, we gain clearer perspective on how much further it may continue developing to drive revenue growth through enhanced customer lifetime value.

The Pre-Digital Era: Contact Management Before Computers

Long before computers, businesses recognized the need to track customer relationships, though primitive tools limited capabilities. The Rolodex, invented in 1956, provided an analog storage solution indexing contacts on rotating cards.

This established concepts of organizing customer names, contact details and interactions that remain relevant despite technological leaps.

As mainframe computers emerged, digital databases unlocked the ability to search, sort and analyze client information more easily. However, early digital systems still focused heavily on simple contact management rather than using data to strategically strengthen customer loyalty.

The Building Blocks in the 1980s-90s

CRM fundamentals coalesced in the 1980s and 90s through two parallel innovations:

1. Contact Management Software

2. Sales Force Automation (SFA)

On the contact management front, applications like ACT! delivered digital replicas of the Rolodex indexing contacts, accounts, activities and deal statuses. Though primarily used by sales teams, these tools foreshadowed organization-wide systems for managing enterprise customer relationships.

Concurrently, SFA technology automated sales tasks like activity tracking, pipeline measurement, and territory alignments that had required extensive manual efforts. By saving time on administrative tasks, reps could invest more into customer interactions. This improved productivity and management visibility.

The convergence of enhanced contact management through CMS tools and process efficiency via SFA formed the foundation for customer relationship management as we now know it.

The Internet Age Arrives: Web-Based CRM Takes Hold

The meteoric rise of the internet from the mid-90s onward necessitated a transition away from on-premises CRM tools. As modern websites enabled digital self-service and e-commerce, customer engagement changed radically. Businesses needed flexible systems adapting to these shifts.

In this environment, the first web-based CRM emerged when Salesforce launched in 1999. This pioneering software-as-a-service (SaaS) model relied on cloud hosting to facilitate anywhere access through browsers. Avoiding cumbersome local app installs, updates and maintenance, web CRM enabled real-time collaboration across distributed teams. Competitors soon followed Salesforce's lead.

This founding web-based CRM delivered key features including:

Contact Management – Complete client profiles integrated from various touchpoints
Lead Management – Assign, track and nurture promising potential opportunities
Reporting & Analytics – Custom reports to illuminate sales insights

While functionality remained quite basic compared to today, these systems fulfilled core CRM needs for many businesses through the early 2000s.

The Rise of Modern Multi-Channel CRM

As internet use expanded drastically across all demographics by 2010, customers engaged brands through an exploding range of digital channels beyond just websites. Modern CRM evolved in parallel to help sales, marketing and support teams engage through avenues like:

- Email Marketing: Design, automate and track personalized email campaigns

- Social Media: Monitor sentiment, respond to comments, and convert followers

- Mobile Apps: Support on-the-go usage with native iOS and Android access

- Live Web Chat: Enable real-time support directly through websites

- Customer Service Portals: Streamline case management via self-service tools

This proliferation of communications modalities made multi-channel integration an imperative. Leading CRM platforms achieved this by:

- Consolidating data across channels into unified client records

- Embedding tools directly in the system interface

- Building application programming interfaces (APIs) to connect specialized third-party apps

With a single dashboard to oversee interactions, teams could coordinate seamlessly to align messaging while gathering robust data to chart customer journeys.

The Role of CRM in Sales Ops

Customer relationship management (CRM) tools have become deeply embedded in the sales process of most organizations. As these systems grow more sophisticated with expansive databases, automation, and analytics, the need for dedicated sales operations professionals to implement and oversee them increases. Without this oversight, ineffective system usage and chaotic, unreliable data are likely outcomes.

CRM and sales operations have grown up together in the business world. As CRM adoption became widespread in the 1990s and 2000s, sales organizations realized the software was too complex for self-guided adoption. Sales operations emerged as a discipline to bridge the gaps between sales teams, technology leaders, and executives.

Early sales operations professionals typically specialized in maximizing CRM utility. Vendor certifications for platforms like Salesforce, Microsoft Dynamics, and SugarCRM became common gateway roles into sales ops. Mastering these tools remains core to the sales operations skill set today.

Leading CRM platforms now integrate extensive capabilities including:

- Databases with customer, prospect, and market data

- Sales process automation tools

- Artificial intelligence and predictive analytics

- Sales activity tracking and performance dashboards

- Customizable reporting and business intelligence

With so many components, Sales Ops oversight is required to actualize and optimize CRM investments. Absent governance and strategic adoption, organizations risk two outcomes:

1. Low or Non-Existent User Adoption: Salespeople become overwhelmed and use the CRM minimally or not at all.

2. Data Chaos: Teams misuse tools leading to incomplete, duplicative, or unreliable data.

Both scenarios significantly limit the CRM value to sales leaders and executives. Dedicated sales operations personnel can prevent these pitfalls via managerial best practices explored throughout this guide.

The modalities of customer relationship management continue advancing rapidly. While exciting innovations emerge constantly, exploiting CRM fully demands specialized oversight to tame the complexities. By investing in sales operations leadership and expertise, organizations can transform disjointed processes into synchronized ecosystems that enhance customer loyalty and sales performance.

Empowering Sales Through Proactive Sales Operations Partnerships

The most effective sales operations teams view sales representatives as their primary customers. Rather than operating as a passive support function, they actively collaborate with salespeople to understand workflow pain points and anticipate helpful solutions. This philosophy transforms sales ops from a cost center into a true force multiplier for revenue growth.

When sales operations takes on the customer service mindset, several benefits emerge:

- Salespeople gain efficiencies by offloading manual tasks and technology headaches. This liberates them to focus energy on revenue-generating activities.

- Staff feel empowered to ideate and innovate knowing that sales ops provides specialized expertise and executive partnership to actualize ideas.

- Management obtains better visibility into field challenges and opportunities without constant middle management reporting.

- The entire organization benefits from enhanced sales productivity, smarter investments in enabling technologies, and ultimately healthier top and bottom-line results.

The highest-performing sales operations leaders view their responsibilities expansively. Beyond fielding one-off sales rep requests, they actively listen, monitor usage patterns, and survey teams to identify critical pain points. With deep understanding of workflows, they can preemptively build solutions to equip sales staff for future periods of rapid growth.

This could involve anything from building custom analytics reports in CRM to help reps segment high-value accounts more effectively to developing educational sales tools to support launching complex new products. By maintaining tight feedback loops with sales teams and thinking ahead to forthcoming needs, sales operations transforms into an invaluable ally.

As selling grows more complex amid shortened sales cycles and expanding competition, successful execution increasingly depends on enabling technologies and specialized expertise. This environment provides a perfect opportunity for sales operations leaders to evolve from reactionary support players into fully integrated and visionary partners. By understanding sales reps as core customers and anticipating their requirements, sales ops can unlock vastly greater organizational potential.

Look Beyond the CRM

While CRM platforms remain foundational sales technologies, the digital transformation mandates a more expansive suite of tools. As sales and marketing converge and buyers self-educate across channels, organizations require integrated technologies to synchronize efforts. Sales operations executives now oversee comprehensive "stacks" spanning CRM, sales engagement, digital content, and more.

This guide examines the expanding sales technology landscape and how sales ops leaders can effectively build, manage, and maximize interconnected system ecosystems. With the right architecture and training strategy powered by people, process, and technology, teams gain flexibility to engage customers anytime, anywhere while capturing robust data for improved forecasting.

While CRM anchors sales technology environments, demand grows for specialized tools in four key areas:

1. Marketing Automation: Integrates CRM data to deliver personalized digital campaigns and content tailored to each stage of the buyer journey.

2. Email Marketing: Enables design and delivery of targeted email content tracked within the CRM record.

3. Sales Engagement: Bridges outreach gaps between marketing automation and sales contacts via customized messaging at scale.

4. Social Media Management: Monitors brand mentions and conversations across social platforms to identify engagement opportunities.

As sales and marketing tools proliferate, sales operations leaders must stitch these technologies together for multiple benefits:

1. Provide consistent CX as customers transition across stages and channels

2. Maintain data integrity and transparency across systems

3. Reduce inefficiencies from manual task repetition

4. Gain holistic visibility through integrated analytics

With the right architecture, sales technology ecosystems enable teams to engage buyers anytime, anywhere while capturing robust data for accurate forecasting and revenue acceleration.

Modern sales technology environments demand deep interconnections to sync critical systems and data. As customer journeys fragment across digital channels, specialized engagement tools continue proliferating rapidly. Sales operations leaders play an indispensable role in architecting ecosystems where platforms communicate freely. With tight integration guided by overarching strategy, organizations can unlock flexibility and insight to drive revenue growth efficiently at scale.

CRM as a Tool to Enhance Customer Loyalty

Modern customer relationship management (CRM) platforms integrate previously disjointed systems to help businesses build customer loyalty. This guide provides practical advice on leveraging CRM to strengthen sales operations and maximize lifetime customer value.

We will demystify essential CRM capabilities, infrastructure options, and implementation best practices. The goal is to empower sales operations leaders to optimize CRM ecosystems for enabling sustainable revenue growth.

Leading CRM platforms on the market offer flexible access models that organizations can choose from based on their preferences and requirements. The three main options are: cloud-based, remotely hosted software-as-a-service solutions; on-premises setups with locally installed servers fully controlled within the organization; and hybrid implementations involving both cloud-based applications and on-site infrastructure. Companies weigh a variety of determining factors when deciding between deployment options, including needs around security, data governance, custom integration capabilities, and more.

CRM consolidation provides indispensable functionality through four main areas: unified customer profiles that compile data from all touchpoints; sales and marketing automation that streamlines repetitive outreach tasks; service case management to track issues from inception through resolution; and custom analytics that provide insights across the entire customer journey. With comprehensive and integrated data views and process workflows, teams across the organization can better coordinate efforts to ultimately drive greater customer loyalty.

Among the most vital components for successfully leveraging CRM include effective IT change management practices through phased rollouts of technology and process changes; comprehensive education for staff across teams that clearly illustrates optimized workflows and system capabilities; and executive leadership buy-in enlisted by presenting strong business case analyses backed by data-driven metrics and ROI impact projections. With focus on these key implementation success factors, interconnected supporting technology, engaged and informed users, and buy-in from decision-making executives, companies gain the necessary foundations to activate CRM's full potential for enhancing customer lifetime value.

As consumer behaviors and systems continuously evolve, specialized expertise maximizes CRM infrastructure. This guide has aimed to condense complexity into accessible advice for leveraging CRM in strategic sales operations roles. With core capabilities, flexible access models, and disciplined adoption protocols, modern platforms promise immense value. We encourage leaders to forge ahead boldly yet deliberately when strengthening the customer-centric technology foundations that sales teams rely upon daily.

Chapter One

Understanding Business Requirements

A customer relationship management (CRM) platform is an invaluable asset for small and medium businesses looking to scale operations and boost bottom lines through superior customer experiences. However, with the sea of solutions available, selecting the right match that aligns to your budget, objectives, and workflows can prove daunting.

Settle on a shortlist of viable CRMs that best satisfy your must-have needs, support key growth objectives, and align to current and future budget realities. From there, thoroughly test drive each system across relevant teams to make an evidence-based final selection. Keeping sight of your critical pain relief targets and aspirations sets you up to choose a customer relationship management platform that propels your business forward.

Identify Your Business Requirements and Obstacles

The foundational step is comprehensively auditing your current sales, marketing and customer service pathways from end-to-end. Document every manual touchpoint, spreadsheet, metric, and team interaction. Look for friction points like siloed data accessibility, disjointed hand-offs between departments, repetitive administrative tasks, and gaps in insight that impair progress.

Define where bandwidth bottlenecks and misalignments reside. Which scenarios reflect the highest opportunity costs from coordination issues and poor visibility? The more granular your understanding of workflow shortcomings, the better equipped you will be to address them through a tailored CRM implementation.

Additionally, note functional areas where your teams currently thrive, like lead qualification procedures or customer onboarding. Identify processes that should remain intact so you avoid disrupting what already works at peak effectiveness when transitioning to new systems. Your optimal CRM magnifies strengths while resolving weaknesses.

Next, detail the specific obstacles hindering your ability to acquire, support and retain customers at scale. Are sales bottlenecked by inadequate lead generation volumes? Is resource-intensive manual follow-up diluting focus on high-potential opportunities? Are customer insights siloed across systems, creating disjointed experiences?

Construct a comprehensive catalog of challenges and rank them by business impact. This clear-eyed accounting of barriers informs which capabilities you need in a solution. For instance, insufficient lead volumes necessitate robust marketing automation while dispersed customer data merits a unified hub for managing interactions. Let your obstacles guide requirements.

With current functionality gaps and pain points established, translate desired improvements into specific, measurable targets reflective of your growth goals. Rather than vague notions of increasing sales, strive for tangible metrics like "boost lead conversion rate from 20% to 30%" or "reduce customer churn by 300 basis points."

An acute focus on quantified desired outcomes ensures any CRM under evaluation can empirically demonstrate a capacity to achieve them through relevant functionality. Whether aiming to double sales team productivity or improve customer satisfaction scores by 40 points, defining precise targets is essential to aligning technology with advancement.

By undertaking an extensive audit of existing processes, obstacles, and targets, you construct a detailed blueprint of needs. Equipped with crystal clarity around required functionalities and desired business impacts, you can rapidly narrow viable CRM options to find the platform primed to solve your biggest challenges and propel progress. The remainder of this guide explores techniques for aligning providers to your specifications.

Determining Your Optimal CRM

Numerous CRM platforms now provide functionalities catered to unique business sectors like real estate, finance, healthcare, and nonprofit. If your processes handle sensitive data or require meeting regulatory compliance standards like HIPAA, only options purpose-built for your vertical can enable continuity without disruption. Carefully analyze industry-specific traits to shortlist sector-specialized market leaders ready to fulfill niche obligations. Their expertise translates into instant optimizations rather than risky reinvention initatives.

Additionally, some systems excel at business-to-business (B2B) relationship building through corporate customer lifecycle management while others focus on business-to-consumer (B2C) sales velocity and consumer marketing. Analyze your prevailing business model - B2B, B2C or a hybrid - to find an intuitive fit.

CRM software spans an array of modules from sales force automation to customer service and marketing campaign management. Pinpoint which teams and functions will leverage the system most. Will it serve as a sales team's hub for nurturing opportunities or empower support agents to resolve service cases?

Highly sales-centered businesses may prioritize lead scoring and pipeline visibility while marketing-driven ones demand campaign tracking and analytics. Defining internal usage ensures the solution scales to current and future process requirements cost-effectively through role-based packages.

Finally, factor in non-negotiable capabilities like calendaring, data accessibility from anywhere, task management and workflows. Other useful items like project collaboration, third-party software integrations and automation maximize value but can be supplemented if the CRM aligns well otherwise. By specifying must-haves versus nice-to-haves, you distill the criteria integral for success.

While the CRM marketplace appears saturated, understanding points of distinction in terms of specialized vertical applicability, business models and internal usage delivers clarity. Prioritizing these strategic dynamics first enables you to confidently narrow options to solutions delivering transformative outcomes through both out-of-the-box and customizable capabilities. The remainder of this guide will explore techniques for evaluating shortlisted CRM systems to finalize the perfect platform positioning your company for enduring customer relationships.

Modern customer relationship management (CRM) platforms consolidate an array of capabilities to overcome previous limitations – clarifying why they are becoming business-critical technologies. CRM software features often consist of:

Centralizing Contact Information

The most fundamental yet invaluable CRM capability is maintaining a centralized database of customer and prospect contact records. Rather than piecing together dispersed data sources like individual email accounts and Excel sheets, a CRM offers a "single source of truth" for up-to-date emails, phone numbers, addresses, company information, and communication/activity histories.

Consolidating this data into individual 360-degree customer profiles eliminates painful manual merging and mailing list exports. More importantly, it lays the foundation for adding layers of rich analytics around your relationships through subsequent capabilities outlined below. Accessing comprehensive, accurate customer profiles from a unified CRM hub proves foundational.

Monitoring Interactions and Activity

Transactional interactions represent the lifeblood of customer relationships. Whether service cases, sales inquiries or email exchanges, tracking various channels and forms of engagement offers a granular window into relationship health.

CRM activity tracking tools automatically log details like interaction dates/times, parties involved, statuses and outcomes. This produces an always up-to-date timeline of communications which teams can review before follow-ups to continue conversations contextually. Over longer periods, aggregated activity sheds light on relationship cadences, channel preferences, and lifecycle stages to inform personalization.

Managing Tasks and Assignments

With customer activity documented, CRMs empower you to facilitate efficient internal coordination through assignments and task management functionalities. Sales leaders can create prospect outreach actions for representatives while support managers delegate case resolutions to agents according to specializations.

Open task queues foster transparency into individual workloads and bottlenecks. Meanwhile, automated reminders via email/text notifications minimize dropped balls. The ability to organize, distribute, monitor and drive tasks related to customer interactions ensures coordinated care.

Structuring Workflows

For transactional processes like purchase orders or service requests, CRMs enable you to model workflows that progress interactions through multi-step procedures efficiently. Much like an assembly line, specialized teams handle respective stages from initiation to fulfillment based on intelligent routing rules.

Structuring workflows eliminates the chaos of ad-hoc triaging and communication from simple requests to intricate cases. Templatizing processes also builds institutional knowledge so interactions resolve reliably even amid staff turnover. The capacity to architect and evolve structured pathways makes task execution remarkably smooth.

Building Project Frameworks

While workflows handle high-velocity repetitive tasks, CRM project management functionalities allow organizations to orchestrate more complex, multi-dimensional initiatives across teams, like developing marketing campaigns. Central hubs with assignable sub-tasks, Gantt chart timelines, file-sharing and consolidated notes enable true collaboration.

Project-focused CRMs also facilitate vital oversight into resource allocation across initiatives to balance workloads. And easily accessible archives of historical projects enable continuous improvement of future endeavors through lessons learned. Where workflows streamline repetitive tasks, project management brings order to intricate, evolving initiatives.

Deriving Actionable Insights

The above tracking abilities compile immense volumes of data pertaining to who customers are and how your teams engage them. CRMs fully unleash the value of this aggregated information through built-in reporting tools or integrations with dedicated business intelligence platforms.

Transforming interaction statistics into interactive dashboards, metrics around lead conversion rates, sales cycle durations, complaint rates and retention deliver powerful visibility that moves the needle. Isolating trends around your best customers informs acquisition priorities while red flags prompt engagement model changes. CRM analytics converts once siloed noise into strategic signals.

By centralizing contacts, interactions, tasks, workflows and projects into CRM hubs and extracting insights through reporting tools, organizations gain unprecedented control over the customer experience. Now the challenge becomes choosing the right platform that aligns to your budget and process characteristics. But the ability to optimize relationships rests on a foundation of CRM capability orchestration.

CRM for Sales Management

When customers expect hyper-personalized buying journeys, creating customized experiences at scale grows increasingly labor-intensive for sales teams striving for efficiency. Furthermore, coordinating with siloed marketing and support functions impedes visibility into relationships as they traverse complex funnels. Sales Ops managers wield CRM platforms as indispensable tools to align internal stakeholders, strengthen understanding, and ultimately empower reps for far greater effectiveness.

Centralizing Data for Powerful Patterns

At their core, CRMs construct rich 360-degree views of customer histories and affinities by unifying data from websites, phones, past orders, case tickets and more. Integrating this information from disparate sources forms complete pictures of individuals and accounts for reps to consume. When grounded in data-driven understanding, they can divert focus from administration to strategic pursuits, such as crafting hyper-personalized outreach and presenting tailored solutions reflective of each company's challenges.

In addition, centralized relationship records enable managers to uncover usage trends, triggers, and future needs across customer cohorts. They gain an eagle-eye vantage point to proactively adjust playbooks, staffing models, and initiatives based on empirical patterns rather than intuition. The CRM becomes a catalyst for continuous improvement rooted in relationship truths.

Orchestrating Efficient Campaign Execution

Beyond housing data, CRMs facilitate efficient campaign execution and lead routing to demand generation programs or Account Executives according to ideal buyer profiles. Through forms, chatbots on your website instantly capture prospect details for immediate follow-up while scoring tools codify qualification criteria to focus reps only on sales-ready targets. Automating previously clumsy hand-offs via structured workflows secured in the CRM boosts velocity dramatically.

With assignments and timelines consolidated in a single project hub instead of scattered emails, CRM-driven orchestration also fosters cross-functional transparency and seamless collaboration between Sales, Marketing and Customer Success teams as opportunities develop. Managers gain ultimate visibility to align strategies, content and messaging while eliminating redundant outreach.

Informing Optimal Actions

As the sales process intensifies, embedded analytics translate activity metrics into tactical insights around optimal actions for closing deals faster. How long do qualified opportunities take to convert with specific reps? Which content drives the most demos booked? Such granularity detects coaching opportunities and underscores what works.

Equally powerful, long-term analysis of win/loss post-mortems fuels continual refinement of risk factor identification within the pipeline. Spotting patterns around successful deal structures also enables managers to establish validated templates for complex sales within the CRM to accelerate intricate deals. Informed strategy conquers guesswork.

By serving as a intelligence backbone bridging silos, codifying best practices, and revealing precision insights, Customer Relationship Management platforms enable Sales Ops leaders to operate their teams with unprecedented clarity and effectiveness. As processes mature in sophistication, the CRM evolves in lockstep as the single source powering optimization.

Achieving Cross-Functional Excellence

Seldom do sales, marketing, and customer support exist in idyllic alignment, collaborating seamlessly to provide cohesive customer experiences. Instead, disconnected software systems and narrowly focused KPIs breed insular departments operating in silos to the detriment of the collective organization and relationships they aim to foster. However, CRM platforms finally offer a remedy to disjointed operations through unified data, shared visibility, and cross-functional workflow harmony.

Centralizing Data for Universal Access

At their core, CRMs consolidate customer information from websites, social media, support cases, and product registrations into a single hub. This provides complete, up-to-date profiles and interaction histories universally accessible rather than trapped within sales spreadsheets or support ticket portals. Marketing gains visibility into lifetime value and channel preferences for sharper audience segmentation while customer service resolves issues contextually based on past conversations. A unified record anchoring coordinated strategy.

Syncing Around Shared Timelines

Further fostering alignment, CRM activity logging tools auto-capture every email, meeting, and call as timestamped entries on relationship timelines. When sales connects with a hot lead, details instantly populate for service agents handling resultant inquiries. Calendar integration similarly enables teams to visualize colleagues' communications with customers and prospects to expedite responses and eliminate redundant outreach. Such real-time synchronization bridges crucial information gaps.

Modeling Collaborative Workflows

With data and timelines synced, CRMs facilitate actual collaborative processes through workflow functionality. For example, when a support case escalates in complexity, instant routing rules trigger guided creation of an internal sales proposal to upsell services. Automatic notifications then kickstart prescripted cycles of cross-departmental tasks moving the customer toward a resolution and contract. Workflows model interdependent processes for frictionless hand-offs.

By serving as the customer data and communication backbone unifying previously scattered teams, CRM software conquers enterprise silos. Sales, marketing, and service adopt a shared orientation revolving around relationship lifecycles rather than just immediate responsibilities. Ultimately this paves the way for orchestrated continuity and positive brand experiences driving enduring loyalty.

Chapter Two

Selecting the Right CRM

I mplementing a Customer Relationship Management platform promises immense opportunity to streamline workflows, bolster customer insights, and align sales and marketing teams for growth. However, the breadth of options and configurations makes selection daunting. This chapter provides an actionable 10-step methodology grounded in best practices for evaluating providers, stakeholder needs, and critical use cases to assure an ideal CRM match positioning your company for enduring customer relationships.

Step 1: Construct a Budget

Selecting a Customer Relationship Management (CRM) system marks a pivotal business investment necessitating diligent budget planning even before assessing specific solutions. By undertaking financial preparedness aligned to strategic growth objectives, you construct an spending framework optimized for maximum ROI rather than guesswork. This detailed guide to budgeting for CRM success explains key considerations across initialization costs, ongoing fees, calculating returns and modeling projected impacts.

Analyzing Current Technology Spend

The first component when forming your budget is consolidating existing software, data and services expenditures across sales platforms, marketing automation tools, business intelligence and more. While some legacy point solutions may transition into a CRM, itemizing all customer-facing technologies provides an accurate baseline for forecasting overall increases versus redirected costs.

Additionally, highlight expensive manual processes and wasted productivity symptomatic of workflow coordination issues a CRM aims to improve. The people-hour and opportunity costs of strained status quos carry real financial burdens making platform improvements a priority.

Factoring Implementation Services

Implementation costs vary greatly depending on the provider selected, number of data sources and users to onboard, ancillary tools needing integration, and customizations required. Some vendors bundle onboarding assistance with licenses at no added fee while others charge hourly consulting rates. When scoping your budget, factor several thousand dollars at minimum for integration, even if you leverage internal resources. Cutting corners here jeopardizes adoption, so allocate adequately.

Modeling Licensing Expenditures

CRM licensing schema range from unlimited user plans with volume tiers to role-based packages and expensive premium add-ons priced per user. Take into account team expansion plans over 3-5 years and calculate total license requirements upfront to inform negotiations. Additionally decide if you want open API development access or platform extensibility requiring additional fees. Licensing represents the bulk of recurring CRM costs so model user counts diligently.

Calculating 5 Year TCO

With discrete cost inputs defined, extrapolate total cost projections over a 5 year horizon accounting for compounding hosting, support and licensing increases. While intimidating initially, projecting total cost of ownership (TCO) over an extended timeframe ensures sufficient long-term budget availability to maximize capabilities and growth unlocked via ongoing platform optimization. Think marathon not sprint.

Setting Executive ROI Expectations

With TCO understood, work cross-functionally to construct projected return timelines across key performance indicators like sales cycle contractions, monthly recurring revenue gains and customer retention boosts directly attributable to CRM capabilities. Leadership teams often have unrealistic expectations around ROI so setting pragmatic milestones grounded in platform functionality alignmentdispels magical thinking. Savvy goal-setting reduces future discouragement.

The most brilliant CRM proves ineffective if executive teams only authorize minimal spend or expect instant results without appreciation for implementation nuances. Undertaking careful preparedness aligned to strategic targets, growth trajectories and tolerant ROI horizons paves the way for Customer Relationship Management success. Financial diligence sets the stage for rich dividends over years not just months.

Step 2: Profile Your User Base

With budget guardrails established, the next strategic priority is assessing and documenting the various roles, responsibilities and requirements of employees across teams set to actively leverage the Customer Relationship Management (CRM) system upon implementation. Not all users interface identically with platforms so capturing persona nuances informs optimal configuration. This guide explores techniques for constructing holistic profiles of your user ecosystem to assure tailored alignment.

Segmenting by Roles

Cross-functionally catalog job titles for every individual needing access including frontline sales representatives, account managers, service agents, marketers, and sales operations directors amongst others. While many boast customer-facing demands, back office users have distinct platform priorities. Distinguishing needs based on responsibilities spotlights opportunities for role-specific customizations down the line so tools become naturally ingrained into respective routines. No two jobs interact identically, so why should their tools?

Determining Access Requirements

Expanding beyond roles, detail precise system capabilities each subset of employees require for core functions like contact record accessing/updating for service agents or proposal building for account executives. Restrict certain features from roles unlikely to utilize them using licenses with deliberately scoped permissions. Setting judicious boundaries based on genuine needs concentrates spend only on value-driving capabilities per person. Access requirements may also influence rollout prioritization when staging complex enterprise onboarding.

Evaluating Technical Proficiencies

User proficiency spectrums ranging from routines relying purely on institutional knowledge to leveraging daily data analysis dashboards also shape successful adoption. Technically adept analysts expect spreadsheet-style interfaces and customization latitude. Meanwhile less technical sales development associates need intuitive navigation and structured data inputs. Blend user profiles across proficiency levels factor considerably into platform assessment around training resource demands vital for ROI realization.

The CRM landscape brims with new niche solutions yearly forcing managers to relearn platforms constantly, so prioritize continuity and usability over bells and whistles. The most powerful system proves ineffective if overly intricate for daily user aptitudes once the novelty fades. Evaluating technical alignment accelerates adoption.

Proactively investigating and documenting the user base across roles, access needs and technical prowess spotlights strategic distinctions for informing platform requirements. So when examining provider options in steps ahead, you make decisions based on workforce realities. With customer data accessibility and process continuity at stake, profiling the people behind the keyboards shapes Customer Relationship Management success.

Step 3: Map Existing Workflows

Before assessing technical requirements or reviewing vendor features, sales operations leaders must intimately understand existing customer-facing workflows across service cases, onboarding processes, upsell conversations and more. Observing actual pathways informs subsequent CRM optimization for either bolstering effective sequences or resolving friction with automation. This guide details techniques to comprehensively map workflows for driving alignment.

Conducting Stakeholder Interviews

Gather workflow insights by directly consulting employees embedded within respective processes. Discuss pain points impaired by poor communication, repetitive administrative tasks or lack of cross-departmental visibility. The qualitative, human-centered truths highlighted in stakeholder interviews spotlight enhancement areas a tailored CRM solution can resolve. However, also pinpoint aspects functioning smoothly you may want preserved rather preserved despite disruptive software overhauls.

Shadowing Common Scenarios

Next, physically shadow employees through common scenarios like inquiry calls with sales prospects or case troubleshooting meetings between service managers and technicians. Witness their organic pathways for fetching customer history records, coordinating with other departments, and translating discussions into logged CRM activity or order requests within legacy platforms. The current state assessment reveals capability gaps within existing hobbled together technology stacks prime for consolidation or upgrades via a modern CRM.

Process Mapping Workflows

Translating insights gathered from interviews and observations, map processes end-to-end encompassing all tools, communications, conditional decisions, and hand-offs between functions inaccurate detail. Look critically at sequences overall for inefficient loops symptomatic of misaligned software systems with repetitive data reentries or constant check-ins to realign due to poor visibility. Such analyses spotlight precisely how integrated CRM software can directly accelerate specific portions of multifaceted workflows.

While high level process awareness provides context, granular pathway documentation pinpoints exactly where new technologies or automation can alleviate coordination headaches or data accessibility bottlenecks currently throttling productivity. The proof lies in the details - when evaluating platform alignment ensure prospective CRMs demonstrably resolve the biggest shortfalls within documented existing workflows. Smooth adoption necessitates obvious existing pain relief not just empty promises of potential. Spend sufficient time upfront assured your ultimate CRM investment drives maximum impact.

Step 4: Set Executive Team Expectations

Beyond workflows and user requirements, achieving Customer Relationship Management (CRM) implementation success hinges profoundly on properly calibrated executive expectations. Leadership teams must appreciate key milestones spanning months not weeks. They must also understand how embedded capabilities directly drive central growth KPIs from contract values to retention. Misaligned anticipations risk future platform abandonment, so this guide details techniques for imparting pragmatic CRM success measures upon leadership and constructing aligned objectives.

Codifying ROI Projections

Finance executives particularly want ROI forecasting grounded in platform functionality realities, not hype. So beyond typical soft productivity metrics, simulate how the CRM's analytical dashboards will help sales managers identify and pursue higher lifetime value customer cohorts. Estimate new monthly recurring revenue attainable through automated renewal reminders with a 6% increase translating to $X million over 12 months.

Extrapolate figures over 2-3 years accounting for compounding contract expansion enabled via retention improvements. Build projections collaboratively so leadership gains hands-on understanding of how CRM success maps to strategic revenue growth in their actual business model's financial context. These insights temper grandiose assumptions.

Plotting Adoption Trajectories

Next convey realistic system adoption trajectories spanning months not days, factoring adequately for perpetual change resistance and ingrained legacy solution habits. Display graphical plots emphasizing the long runway typically needed for companywide usage saturation, referral levels, and ultimately the workflow transformations enabling forecasted profitability gains. With clarity that daily utilization rates will remain unimpressive initially before compounding, leadership has patience for sustained results.

Formalizing Milestones

Further grounding executive mental models in reality, outline all deployment dependencies from enterprise software integrations finalizing to staff training completions needing phase gating before unlocking full solution access and distribution. Highlight how pockets of power users will pilot the platform and provide feedback cycles before companywide onboarding. Milestones demonstrate the meticulous orchestration underpinning traction.

Right-sizing anticipations requires adjusting against overzealous beliefs that CRMs foster instant, easy enterprise transformations. They certainly enable sales productivity revolutions but only through deliberate change management and capability alignment specific to the organization's commercial context. Savvy sales operations leaders set the tone early through pragmatic forecasting, adoption setting, and milestone planning so teams sustain focus on long-term wins.

Step 5: Audit Existing Software Stack

Legacy software investments encompassing marketing automation, custom analytics, and point channel engagement solutions represent some of the biggest impediments to seamless Customer Relationship Management (CRM) alignment. Yet their embeddedness across teams necessitates integration support. This guide details optimal techniques for auditing existing stacks to inform consolidation and data migration planning to assure continuity amid change.

Cataloging All Technologies

The foundation of any legacy solution audit is an accurate registry of all customer-facing apps and services with corresponding capabilities, stakeholders relying on each, and criticality rankings. Note platforms like chat widgets driving significant inquiries, campaign trackers informing outreach prioritization and custom analytics quantifying team performance. Capture usage scenarios, data types integrated, and key features leveraged daily.

Additionally, distinguish functions served adequately versus pain points like sales/service disjointedness that merit replacement by a unified CRM. Auditing holistically highlights precise transition sequences needed to maintain departmental efficacy amid changes plus capabilities still requiring supplementation like predictive lead scoring.

Scrutinizing Data Infrastructure

An inventory of softwareProvides crucial yet incomplete context lacking the underlying data infrastructure bindings enabling system interoperability. So document interfaces ranging from APIs to file transfer mechanisms driving exchanges across tools along with corresponding formats for contacts, interactions, campaigns and more.

Will the CRM natively consolidate certain platforms or require ongoing integrations? Shining light on these information highways and destinations spotted enhancement areas to fortify with migrations or middleware. Do not underestimate infrastructure's significance.

Calculating Switching Costs

Further analyze financial switching costs posed by existing vendor contracts, such as months remaining on legacy CRM licenses plus negotiated savings entitled upon renewals that may require forfeiting. Balancing timing of upcoming renewal deadlines while claiming entitlements before cutting over shapes transition sequencing and cost mitigation. You avoid platform overlaps burning unnecessary budget.

The audit process grants implementing teams immense clarity regarding longstanding solution shortcomings and data flow opportunities modern CRM solutions can comprehensively resolve if adequately informed by intricacies of current-state stacks. Taking an inventory establishes the foundation for transformation blueprints and guides future investment prioritization.

Step 6: Define Reporting Requirements

Among the most pivotal yet overlooked components when evaluating Customer Relationship Management (CRM) solutions is confirming embedded reporting and analytics capabilities scale to leadership visibility needs around trends, projections, and business performance insights necessary for data-driven decisions and growth planning. This guide discusses techniques for codifying precise measurable reporting requirements upfront to assure CRM alignment.

Modeling Executive Decision Metrics

Cross-functionally consult leadership to construct a comprehensive catalog of essential indicators, statistics, and performance indexes consumed regularly for functions like opportunity pipeline financial forecasting, customer retention program efficacy quantification, or service level trending. Pinpoint the exact CRM analytics and calculated fields translating source activity into vital output measures empowering both operational and strategic moves.

Common examples include monthly recurring revenue metrics factoring multi-year contract values, customer lifetime value indexes demonstrating loyalty program returns, and quarterly sales win rate trends informing territory realignment. Determine which decisions rely on customer insights to model precise scorecards and dashboards your CRM must deliver.

Plotting Historical Data Availability

In conjunction with reporting needs, assess available volumes of historical customer, transactional, product catalogs and other records in legacy systems for porting to the new CRM to assure sufficient analytical depth. While importing 3 years of order data fuels accurate forecasts, many lack information integrity beyond 12-18 months. Plotting availability timeframes allows administrators to set leadership expectations about when rich longitudinal visibility matures following deployment.

Certifying Statistical Models Align

For advanced machine learning offerings like predictive lead scoring, ensure prospective CRMs leverage compatible modeling methodologies aligned to your data types for continued accuracy gains post-migration Avoid sudden drops in robustness! Fine print matters when replacing analytics tools so allow technical experts to validate continuity.

While core CRM architecture generally satisfies common reporting expectations, specialty dashboards leveraged by leadership teams command additional scrutiny around advanced measures. Clearly documenting exact specifications aligned to regular strategic routines and backed by technical due diligence sets the CRM relationship up for enduring decision-making success.

Step 7: Detail Security Obligations

Among the most pivotal yet overlooked components when evaluating CRM solutions is confirming embedded safeguards and access controls sufficiently satisfy both company security policies and industry regulatory compliance obligations for your business vertical. Neglecting to detail precise protections early risks disruption, audit penalties and lost customer trust from data incidents. This guide explores techniques for codifying security and compliance standards upfront to assure CRM preparedness.

Itemizing Sensitive Data Categories

While contact records and interactions comprise typical system data types, specify any additional sensitive information like personal health details for healthcare providers or proprietary performance records a vendor may store necessitating encryption, access restrictions and handling procedures guided by laws like HIPAA or internal protocols. Itemizing regulated data ensures appropriate protections are interrogated.

Spotlighting High-Risk Scenarios

Expand beyond data types to document high-risk usage scenarios requiring safeguards like reps accessing full customer profiles from personal mobile devices or customer service teams integrating payment systems into the CRM for streamlined billing support. Outlining risky yet essential activities informs security evaluations around remote access controls, role-based permissions and financial data protections criticial for continuity.

Mandating Employee Security Training

Detail requirements for comprehensive employee security training upon on-boarding encompassing proper access protocols, safe external usage, phishing threat detection and general data handling best practices in line with company guidelines. Specify any specialized vertical training obligations such as health-care privacy certifications. Mandating instruction spotlights vendor alignment and platform configurability to ingrain conscientious data usage companywide.

While information security ranks low on priority lists for many CRM buyers seduced by feature promises, establishing clear security and compliance standards upfront ensures every vendor under consideration boasts capable data governance to maintain stability through inevitable breaches on the horizon. Taking preventative measures withstands disruptive fines, lawsuits and losses down the line. Due diligence defends customer relationships.

Step 8: Shortlist Provider Options

With strategic priorities spanning optimized budgets, user workflows, infrastructure interoperability, leadership visibility requirements and security policies collectively detailed, sales operations leaders can swiftly filter the expansive CRM marketplace around alignment to these precise specifications. This guide details an effective evaluation methodology enabling teams to generate a capabilities-aligned shortlist optimized for product testing.

Researching the Marketplace

Commence market research spanning industry analyst publications, software review websites, conference vendor showrooms and peer recommendation channels. Catalog CRM providers with the greatest momentum and client representation within your company's size band and vertical. However, rather than reviewing generalized ratings thus far, navigate directly to sections detailing alignment to budget parameters, technology integration options, and key features like workflow and analytics tools set forth in earlier planning stages. Research guided strictly by defined requirements narrows the playing field significantly from thousands to a mere handful meeting qualification standards and merit deeper evaluation. Resist the temptation to excessively broaden initial scope.

Requesting Product Demonstrations

Once a target list emerges spanning 3-5 providers satisfying outlined capability and infrastructure integration imperatives while aligning to executive spending comfort zones, initiate demos. Come armed with specific user workflows, reporting samples, and technical specification documents in hand to interrogate precise platform alignment systematically. Revisit key software architecture questions around data models, API capabilities etc and determine which vendors confirm capabilities through showcases not just promises before your eyes. Demos quickly reveal depth behind marketing.

Checking References

Lastly, verify promising vendor validity through reference checks with companies of similar scale or verticals to affirm satisfactory reliability and support experiences, total cost realities beyond flashy proposals as well as workload requirements for maximizing platform utility. Speaking with actual executives who navigated implementations spotlights critical nuances training courses and demo reels conveniently exclude. Complete the last mile of due diligence before making irreversible selections.

Resisting initial hype stimulation by anchoring selection solely around thoroughly defined essentials, sales operations teams can swiftly generate a focused shortlist of proven CRM aligned to genuine business requirements often obscured by industry buzz. Aligned platforms drive exponential impact when grounded in reality.

Step 9: Evaluate Shortlist Fit

Armed with a targeted shortlist of leading Customer Relationship Management (CRM) providers demonstrably capable of addressing critical workflow efficiency, infrastructure integration, analytics visibility and budget requirements, sales operations leaders must facilitate extensive testing across relevant users and data environments. This guide details optimal evaluation approaches allowing comprehensive solutions scrutiny before eight-figure investment commitments.

Modeling User Testing Environments

Beyond superficial capabilities awareness via screenshots, evaluating teams require live solution access configured to current workflow and data specimens for authentic examination. Have vendors set up sandbox environments modeling integrated legacy systems populated withanonymized yet true-to-life sample contact, activity history and Salesforce automation records. Provision access to relevant sales operations, account executives and service agents to organically test complex routing rules, dashboard drilling and reporting exports mirroring daily routines. Realistic testing conditions assure accurate assessments.

Piloting Workflow Transition Scenarios

Within mirrored environments, establish testing scenarios reflecting workflows primed for optimization like lead assignment processes or service case escalation hand-offs needing streamlining. Have platform admins walk through proposed rule creation while teams probe ease of building extensions, querying abilities and notification comprehensiveness as compared to current workflows. Press vendors to demonstrate precise transition bridging versus theoretical customization traps.tangibility separates contenders.

Staging Data Migration Mock Runs

The most strategically critical evaluation step centers on data migration readiness. Many CRMs promise seamless integrations yet crumble when heavy database transition commences. Stage test runs importing and merging representative data volumes from across current systems including historical records to validate mapping, duplication handling and interface preservation. Leverage technical resources to probe around data model alignments. Deliberate dry runs affirm go-live readiness beyond superficial pledges.

While platform differentiation mostly resides in configurability not base functionality these days, precisely simulating proposed integrations, workflows and data handling on shortlisted CRMs provides empirical confidence beyond procedural guesswork on who truly aligns for acceleration. Rigorous examination protects against crippling investments.

Step 10: Finalizing an Aligned CRM Selection

Upon conclusively evaluating leading proposals and passing technical due diligence inspection, sales operations leaders arrive at the culminating juncture for Customer Relationship Management platform modernization - ratifying a single provider for swift requisition based on alignment to thoroughly validated specifications. This guide discusses techniques for finalizing selections, negotiating favorable terms and paving the implementation runway critical at investment finalization.

Revisiting Defined Requirements

Committee finalist debates often devolve into feature scope creeping and unrealistic customization discussions disconnected from validated needs. So revisit original workflow efficiency opportunities, infrastructure integration plans and user profiling documents grounds decisions in strategic priorities not hypothetical functionality. Evaluate finalist scores based on demonstrated requirement satisfaction across planning materials. Who definitively confirms executability? The rest deserves dismissal.

Negotiating Favorable Terms

Enter final contacts armed with pricing range insights from peer reference checks, total cost of ownership projections, and multi-year roadmaps to secure favorable commercial models spanning discounted user licensing costs, service credits and subscription increases capped to inflation rates. Many sales executives possess authority for sizable concessions to win complex deals. Come fortified with facts and alternates to coax compromises, not bluffs easily detectable.

Reconfirming Scope Containment

As contract negotiations advance, reaffirm scope adhere strictly to mandated "must-haves" defined early on, resisting executive drift towards "nice to have" feature bloat jeopardizing user adoption or blowing near term budgets. Obtain signed authorizations freezing specifications for the initial phase as contracts undergo legal scrutiny. Locking scope secures solution focus so capabilities evolve aligned to value not novelty chase.

With a final selection officially ratified, leadership tensions give way to execution pressures ensuring meticulous launch success. But the CRM evaluation journey's countless judgment junctions consistently anchored by requirements and measures of genuine alignment established the foundation to realize operational transformation. Now realization hinges on change management within complex multi-phase implementation. But choosing the right platform partner paves the way.

Chapter Three

Implemeting the CRM

Implementing a CRM is the process of getting your new CRM platform fully set up and integrated so you and your team can use it to strengthen customer relationships and boost sales performance. This involves more than just plugging in the software and clicking a few buttons. An effective CRM implementation requires research, planning, data migration, integration with other systems, user training, and testing to ensure seamless adoption across your organization.

Approaching these tasks without a plan in place is invites wasted time, confusion, and lost revenue down the line if your CRM ends up poorly aligned to your business needs. That's why crafting a comprehensive CRM implementation plan is mission-critical right from the start.

The Benefits of Investing in Implementation Planning

An investment in thoughtful CRM implementation planning pays invaluable dividends over the long run by setting your organization up for maximum value and impact from your CRM. Here are some of the top reasons to dedicate time upfront to mapping out your implementation approach:

Alignment - A strong implementation plan helps ensure tight alignment between your CRM and specific business objectives around customer relationships, sales productivity, data accuracy, and more. This enables you to track meaningful metrics and demonstrate ROI.

Efficiency - With a structured plan, all stakeholders are coordinated, milestones and testing are defined, and duplicative work is avoided. This accelerates your CRM rollout and adoption.

Data Integrity - An implementation blueprint explicitly addresses how to cleanly migrate legacy data into your new CRM to maintain data accuracy and continuity.

Adoption - Change management, training, and testing processes built into the implementation plan ease user adoption by acclimating employees to the CRM early on.

In summary, an investment in robust planning is an investment in the success of your CRM itself. Much like building a house, you can't cut corners on the blueprint and foundations without running into problems when it comes time to live there. Spending the necessary time mapping out CRM implementation in advance saves tremendous headaches later on while maximizing results.

Crafting a CRM Implementation Plan

Deploying a new CRM without a robust implementation strategy in place courts disappointment, adoption issues, and wasted investment. However, with so much complexity spanning integration coordination, data migration, vendor selection, rollout scheduling, and end user enablement, it's tempting for sales operations leaders to shortchange planning and "just get the tool live."

Resist that urge.

The truth is CRM performance potential directly corresponds to implementation strategy rigor. By investing diligently upfront in core frameworks spanning business analysis, solution evaluation, deployment roadmapping, data migration, system integration, and training, you erect an unshakeable foundation upholding your CRM for years to come.

Conversely, taking shortcuts in foundational planning sabotages success before you even get started. Like building a home, flaws in underlying blueprints undermine the integrity of the eventual structure.

Laying the Groundwork with Business Analysis & Selecting the Right Platform with Solution Evaluation

Kicking off any new CRM implementation starts with getting clarity on where your business is starting from today. Conducting a detailed analysis of your existing customer relationship processes, data, workflows, systems, metrics, and constraints enables you to map out priorities and requirements for an upgraded CRM solution.

Taking the time upfront to thoroughly test and validate CRM solutions sets you up to choose and deploy the ideal platform tuned to your organization's needs. This has been covered in the previous chapter.

Mapping Your Rollout with a Deployment Roadmap

With a CRM selected, putting together a granular deployment roadmap is next to orchestrate each stage of implementation from proof of concept to full production rollout. This sequenced plan of attack details exactly what gets done when, why, and by whom.

Core elements to define within your roadmap include:

- Implementation stages spanning proofs of concept, pilots, targeted departmental rollouts, and eventual companywide deployment

- All key activities and milestones within each stage

- Testing processes to validate functionality, integrations, data migration, workflows, compliance, ease of use, and performance scalability

- Rollback contingency protocols if testing reveals blocking issues

- Owner assignments across business, CRM vendor, IT, project management, and change management teams

- Go/no-go decision gates before advancing each successive stage

Your roadmap both drives day-to-day project execution as well as provides visibility for leadership on progress made versus the plan. Maintaining a single source of truth for rollout status ensures alignment and accountability across what can easily become a fragmented effort involving many moving parts.

Assembling an All-Star Implementation Squad

The most brilliant CRM solution and elaborately mapped rollout mean nothing without an adept implementation taskforce orchestrating your transition. Handpicking a blended team of project managers, subject matter experts, IT specialists, trainers, and power users to shepherd deployment breeds success.

Project managers anchor the squad, driving workstreams and dependencies in alignment with your meticulously plotted roadmap. Subject matter experts immersed in your customer operations supply know-how on translating processes into configurations.

IT resources provision infrastructure, administer security protocols, and oversee integrations. Dedicated trainers prepare materials and deliver orientation sessions tailored to different users and abilities. Finally, influential users across business units provide ground-truth feedback, champion adoption, and validate functionality.

This cross-functional troupe moves in lockstep, ensuring nothing slips between the cracks. Relying solely on vendors or IT often produces gaps disconnected from commercial outcomes. Supplement them with business-rooted expertise.

Continuously survey milestones versus your master blueprint so momentum carries you swiftly to the finish line. An implementation team meeting its marks manifests ROI rapidly. Choose members wisely and invest in their readiness

Establishing a Data Bridge with Migration Execution

With solution evaluation, roadmap alignment, and integration planning resolved, the time comes to populate your shiny new CRM with the lifeblood of sales and marketing: data. As called out earlier, constructing a robust data migration plan is mandatory. Now you must execute that vision.

Your migration scripts, routines, or services bridge the gap connecting legacy data stores into your new platform. Account information, opportunity pipelines, customer interaction logs, transaction archives, prospect profiles, automation rules, and more journey across the divide.

Meticulously orchestrating this movement sustain continuity while preventing gaps or losses resulting from misaligned mapping, scheduling quirks, or sync failures. Verifying completeness and accuracy of transferred records through query spot-checks and reporting compares safeguards go-live integrity.

Ideally, migrations occur in stages aligned to deployment waves, not overnight cutovers. This enables verification of early data sets. CRM providers often assist migration approaches as part of onboarding.

While arduous, perfecting data flow into the new CRM unlocks organizational adoption and impact. Teams can only execute game plans if the full playbook makes it into the system. Take control of your data bridge.

Safeguarding Data Integrity with Migration Planning

The backbone of any successful CRM is quality customer data. That's why constructing a robust data migration plan within your implementation blueprint is non-negotiable. This plan details how you'll transfer legacy customer, prospect, transaction, interaction, and sales performance data into your new CRM without compromising integrity, continuity, or visibility.

Putting in the work upfront to "clean" existing data by deduplicating, correcting, standardizing, and enriching records saves endless headaches down the line. Legacy data mapping and conversion routines configured preceding go-live provide peace of mind that nothing falls between the cracks once migration occurs.

Your data migration plan also addresses pivotal considerations like minimization of downtime, user access and permissions continuity, transaction loss prevention, and re-establishment of automated workflows.

While often overlooked, prioritizing data migration strategy makes or breaks CRM adoption and trust in the new solution from Day 1. Plan accordingly.

Harmonizing Systems with Integration Planning

Beyond housing data itself, your CRM also needs to interoperate bi-directionally with surrounding sales and marketing systems to foster adoption. That's why defining integration touchpoints with complementary tools like email, phone, ecommerce, payments, and marketing automation underpins usage.

This interplay enables triggering actions in one system based on behaviors in another, eliminating repetitive manual entry and keeping data in sync across your technology stack.

Your integration plan maps out:

- All required integration points between the CRM and adjacent tools

- Data to be shared across systems

- Trigger logics in both directions

- Testing protocols to validate syncing before go-live

- Contingency plans for intermittent connectivity failures

Getting integrations right seals gaps across point solutions. The time invested avoiding integrations as an afterthought or scramble during deployment protects productivity.

Getting Employees Up to Speed with Training Frameworks

Finally, even the most perfectly designed CRM solution fails when users don't understand how to properly leverage it or resist usage altogether. That's why implementing comprehensive change management and training frameworks as part of your rollout plan promotes willingness and capability to adopt the new tools.

Training curriculum tailored to different functions and skill levels accelerates proficiency. Hands-on simulations and sandboxes mimicking real-world application foster confidence. Reinforcing usage through manager accountability provides motivation.

Make training and change management fixed stops on your implementation journey, not bolted-on afterthoughts. Doing so cements employee buy-in and expertise to fully harness your CRM's potential from the outset.

Approaching CRM implementation without structured business analysis, solution evaluation, deployment roadmapping, data migration planning, integration design, and training processes in place flirts with disjointed, shallow adoption ultimately wasting resources. Defining these core components upfront and revisiting them vigilantly throughout your rollout journey protects success, productivity, and ROI. Great strategy builds great CRM performance - tackle that blueprint first.

Communicating Clearly Throughout the Journey

Even the most surefooted CRM deployment stumbles without proactive change management engaging everyone impacted across implementation waves.

Failing to sustain open lines of communication inviting input and questions breeds misinformation, confusion, resistance, and anxiety that stall adoption.

Get ahead of these risks by overcommunicating throughout every project stage. Sales and customer operations brass should host periodic town halls socializing progress to date, next milestones, and how teams should prepare. Concise email newsletters reinforce updates.

Make transparency core to your rollout culture. Loop cross-functional leaders into planning sessions to broaden perspectives. Conduct pilot groups to gather direct user feedback rather than decide policies in a vacuum.

Welcome constructive criticism, advice, and ideas from the front lines pre-, mid-, and post-deployment. Sales and services teams feeling involved gain a sense of ownership, not overnight disruption forced upon them.

Care and feeding of your people minimizes speed bumps so technology and process changes stick. Simply installing a CRM will not trigger benefits - rallying hearts, minds, and hands around it will. Keep everyone in the loop.

Validating CRM ROI and Impact

The final plays in any winning CRM game plan focus on quantifying returns on the considerable time, talent, and technology investments made. With your solution live and stabilized after months of Herculean coordination lifting it over the goal line, now examine evidence of business impact.

Revisit those vital key performance indicators (KPIs) outlined during initial solution evaluation and business analysis planning. Metrics around sales outcomes, forecast accuracy, customer retention, engagement rates, deal cycle compression and more indicate if your CRM deployment is delivering its promised punch.

Leverage native reporting dashboards along with manual audits assessing user adoption levels, data quality, and automation leakage. Voice of customer surveys and interviews inject user perspectives into success measures.

If targets are being met, celebrate wins with those pivotal players who turned strategy into an operational slam dunk. If gaps exist, revisit configurations, integrations, training, and workflows to remix and improve.

Either way, resist set-it-and-forget-it mentalities. Your CRM, and implementation blueprint supporting it, evolve perpetually. Squeeze maximum value through continuous checks driving enhancements over time. Stay analyzing.

Realistic CRM Implementation Timeframes

When embarking on a new CRM implementation, one key question sales operations leaders justifiably ask is "how long will this take?" Unfortunately, there's no universal timeline applying to all deployments. Several variables affect how rapidly you can activate your new CRM solution. Factors such as company size, integration complexity, customization needs, data volumes, and training scale all sway time investments.

Additionally, while eager sales teams may pressure you to "flip the switch" ASAP, resist taking shortcuts. Attempting overly aggressive rollout schedules risks user adoption, functionality gaps, spotty data, and abandoned usage down the line if milestones get missed.

Keeping these dynamics in mind, what are realistic time expectations to set across typical CRM implementation scenarios? Here are some informed benchmarks:

Basic CRM for Small Business: 4-8 Weeks – For a lightweight deployment with minimal customization, integrations, or migrated data, target one to two months. After vendor selection and configuration sprints, small teams can ramp up quickly.

Moderate CRM for Mid-Market Company: 8-16 Weeks – For more complex environments tightly integrating finance systems and larger data sets, plan for two to four months. Building integrations, configuring security, migrating data, and testing end-to-end functionality takes time.

Custom Enterprise-Grade CRM: 16+ Weeks – Finally, highly customized platforms typically demand four months or longer, especially when tailored intensely to complex sales processes. Rigorous security, scaling, and regression testing also lengthen validation.

The key is mapping dependencies and padding buffer rather than projecting (or hoping for) best-case duration. Establish realistic milestones for every project stage to keep stakeholders aligned on pace.

Accelerating Outcomes with Agile Governance

Despite these general benchmarks, all teams rightfully aim to accelerate viable CRM access. Agile governance frameworks promote speed by breaking implementations into rapid, iterative deployments versus monolithic projects. This agile approach rolls out capabilities in waves prioritized by business value. Tight feedback loops keep solutions evolving per user needs. Simultaneous testing and development expedite usable functionality.

So while months-long transformations may seem unavoidable, nimble methods and mindsets inject pace and flexibility relative to more rigid waterfall initiatives. Empower your team to start small but iterate quickly.

Typical CRM implementation timeframes span one to six months depending on scope. But outcomes matter more than output. Savvy IT and sales ops leaders beat the clock through agile delivery focused on fast results versus large, lumbering software builds. Right-size the schedule, then accelerate in sprints.

Chapter Four

Customizing Your CRM for Sales Success

T o drive sales performance, your CRM system needs to empower your teams rather than restrict them. The right CRM customizations can help sales reps and managers work smarter by streamlining processes, improving data flows, and enhancing customer interactions. With some thoughtful configuration guided by your organization's unique needs, you can transform an out-of-the-box CRM into an invaluable asset for sales growth.

Tailoring Workflows for Sales Efficiency

Automating repetitive tasks is one of the best ways to help sales teams work more efficiently. By customizing workflows in your CRM, you can ensure no valuable selling time is wasted on administrative busywork.

For instance, you could create an automated workflow to assign new leads to reps based on territory, instantly notify reps of new assignments via email, and schedule follow-up tasks for initial outreach. Such workflow automation keeps lead response times low while freeing up reps to focus on actual selling activities.

You can also customize workflows to standardize your unique sales processes. For example, if your sales cycle requires multiple prospect meetings and manager approvals, you can map out each step as an automated workflow within your CRM. This way, reps always know the next play and managers have visibility into deals progressing through the pipeline.

Capturing the Right Data

To gain helpful insights from your CRM, you need to make sure it captures all the customer and deal data that is most important to your sales organization. Carefully reviewing standard CRM entities like contacts, accounts, opportunities, and activities can reveal gaps where custom fields may be required.

For instance, you may want to track contract renewal dates, add a field on the account for customer lifetime value, or include a deal risk score on opportunities. By tailoring data fields and values to your specific business needs, you enable better reporting, forecasting, and analytics. You also improve data quality by mapping information correctly from the start.

Enhancing the Customer Experience

A customized CRM strategy focused on understanding customers and improving interactions can be a competitive differentiator for sales teams. Small tweaks to entities like contacts and accounts can uncover data that helps reps personalize outreach and provide better service.

For example, adding custom fields to store key customer details like communication preferences, previous purchases, or outstanding support tickets allows your reps to reference that context during sales calls. Updated opportunity fields could also notify reps when customers approach renewal dates or major milestones. Such customizations ultimately strengthen customer relationships and loyalty.

With some thoughtful planning guided by your organization's needs and processes, purposeful CRM customization allows sales teams to work smarter.

The right configurations and automations provide the foundation for enhanced productivity, actionable data, and improved customer experiences—ingredients for sales success.

Importance of customizing a CRM for sales strategy

In today's highly competitive selling environment, an impactful sales strategy is imperative for business growth. While off-the-shelf customer relationship management (CRM) systems offer robust core functionality, customization can unlock a strategic advantage by optimizing your CRM for your unique sales processes and objectives. With thoughtful enhancements guided by your organization's needs, you can transform your CRM into an invaluable asset for executing and amplifying your sales strategy.

The foundation of a successful sales strategy is a keen understanding of your ideal customers, their buyer journeys, and how to guide them from prospect to loyal client. An out-of-the-box CRM provides standard tools for tracking contacts, accounts, and deals, but lacks the specificity required to capture the customer insights you need to inform sales strategy.

By taking the time to map your sales processes and identify key data points, you can determine where CRM customization is needed to support strategic goals. For example, you may require custom entities to house market research on customer demographics or intelligence on competitors vying for the same deals. Enhanced reporting dashboards could also highlight sales metrics you want to track and trends needing intervention.

Realizing the Full Potential of CRM

Most businesses today rely on CRM systems to manage sales processes, pipeline visibility, and customer interactions. Yet the full potential of CRM to accelerate revenue growth often goes unrealized due to inflexible, one-size-fits-all platforms lacking strategic customization. With thoughtful enhancements tailored to your sales organization's unique processes, objectives and culture, you can optimize your CRM to help drive sales performance.

This section explores key customization areas to consider for transforming an ordinary CRM into an invaluable asset powering sales excellence. We'll cover proven ways to:

- Streamline workflows around your sales methodology for operational efficiency

- Enrich data capture to inform sales strategy decisions

- Equip sales reps to execute high-impact selling activities

- Create visibility to demonstrate sales strategy ROI

Let's explore tips within each area to help you shape a customized CRM that catapults sales success.

Automating Workflows for Sales Process Efficiency

For many sales teams, ineffective lead response processes and administrative tasks bog down productivity. Customized workflows within your CRM can alleviate these inefficiencies through automation and by standardizing best-practice selling motions.

For example, workflow rules can automatically route new leads to reps based on territory, ideal customer profile, or specialization for prompt follow-up. Email templates enable one-click personalized outreach while tasks keep rep activities aligned to proven pipeline progression practices.

Deal stage workflows move opportunities through sales stages matching your established sales methodology. Configurable approval chains for discounts or proposals also enforce consistency for deal standards.

With thoughtful workflow planning and automation guided by your unique sales processes, you gain operational efficiencies allowing reps to focus time on selling rather than manual administration.

Enriching Data to Inform Sales Decisions

Leveraging CRM data to maximum impact depends on capturing the right information at the right time. Standard out-of-the-box entities often lack fields, values and relationships specific to your offerings, customers and processes.

Enriching data requires a deep look at what additional intelligence could help inform sales strategy and tactics. For example, key account managers may want to track renewal or expansion opportunities approaching within existing customers. This could merit new custom fields on Accounts and Contacts showing renewal dates, contract value and a retention score.

Enhanced Contacts might also store communication preferences, consumable usage data, or outstanding support tickets to help reps personalize messaging. Activity customizations could allow tagging customer meetings, events or emails to specific sales programs for better campaign analytics.

Such targeted data customizations build a 360-degree customer view that reveals triggers for new sales conversations and helps align tactical activities to overarching sales objectives around profitability, renewals, penetration or retention.

Empowering Sales Reps with Custom Tools

Even with strong sales strategy and operations, success hinges on frontline sales reps skillfully executing high-value activities. Unfortunately, rigid out-of-the-box CRM functionality often hinders field selling productivity.

Customization here involves identifying impediments to sales execution based on rep feedback, then configuring tailored tools and real-time data access to address pain points. Examples include customized guided selling templates facilitating discovery calls or automated field activity capture from mobile devices to eliminate manual entry.

You can also amplify sales enablement through quick access links, pushing relevant knowledge articles based on opportunity stage or account profile. Similarly, enhancing Activity feeds or Chatter with alerts around key customer developments keeps reps selling insight top of mind.

Such enhancements eliminate technology adoption friction while serving reps critical customer intelligence when and where they need it to progress opportunities. Empowered sales teams who can seamlessly execute your sales methodology ultimately convert more pipeline into closed business.

Gaining Visibility into Performance

As a sales leader, real-time visibility into metrics aligned to strategic KPIs is essential for understanding what's working and rapidly adjusting playbooks as needed. This is where customized analytics, dashboards and embedded reporting truly earn their value.

For example, executive dashboards featured targeted lead conversion rates, sales cycle or activity quota attainment help quickly gauge operational health. Manager dashboards could display team attainment of revenue targets or identify low perfuming reps for coaching. Rep dashboards might show individual quota attainment and activity progression against peers.

Customized opportunity reports can also reveal sales stage conversion rates, win probability scores, or average deal sizes to inform pipeline assumptions. For post-sales analysis, custom reports could break down performance by product line, deal source, age of account or other dimensions you want to track.

This tailored analytics layer translates activity data into actionable insights leaders need to course correct strategy, while demonstrating bottom-line impact.

As we've explored, an adaptable CRM solution tailored to your organizational requirements through purposeful enhancements can truly transform sales performance. When technology directly supports established sales processes and objectives, efficiencies improve, teams access key intelligence, and leaders gain informed visibility to accelerate growth.

However, customization success requires an iterative, user-centric approach accounting for unique team workflows. Quickly implementing a dozen new fields or objects without input often backfires through poor adoption. Ongoing feedback mechanisms are key, along with change management support addressing data, system and selling behavior adjustments.

With a thoughtful roadmap and change enablement mindset guided by clearly defined sales strategy aims, you can mold your CRM into an invaluable asset driving higher revenue – and confidently demonstrate the ROI.

Optimizing Your CRM for Sales Growth

Most businesses rely extensively on CRM systems to manage sales operations, pipeline visibility, and customer interactions. However, rigid out-of-the-box CRM platforms often fail to address unique business needs, resulting in inefficient processes and lost revenue opportunities.

With thoughtful customization guided by your sales organization's specific requirements, you can transform an ordinary CRM into an invaluable asset accelerating team productivity, deal flow, and sales growth. Let's explore key areas ripe for enhancement.

Streamlining Workflows

Ineffective lead response protocols and manual administrative tasks drain selling time for many sales teams. Customized workflows within your CRM can alleviate these productivity killers through automation and standardized best-practice selling motions.

For example, workflow rules could automatically route new leads to reps based on territory, ideal customer profile, or specialization for prompt follow-up. Email templates enable personalized, one-click outreach while automatically generated tasks keep rep activities aligned to proven pipeline progression practices.

Deal stage workflows move opportunities through a sales process matching your methodology and instill discipline around required steps for proposal approvals, discount requests, or prospect meetings. Thoughtful workflow planning around your unique rhythms takes repetition off reps' plates so they can focus time on selling.

Enriching Data

Getting strategic insights from CRM data depends on capturing the right information at key process points. As out-of-the-box entities often lack fields specific to your offerings, customers and processes, enriching data requires a deep analysis of intelligence gaps your teams need to inform sales decisions and tactics.

For example, account managers may want to track upcoming subscription renewals and expansion opportunities within existing customers through new custom fields on Accounts showing renewal dates, contract value tiers, or retention risk scores.

Enhanced Contacts could store preferred communication channels, key customer metrics like ordering history or support ticket volume, and personal details to help reps personalize messaging for enhanced engagement.

Such targeted, role-based data customizations build a 360-degree customer view that reveals triggers for sales conversations and helps align activities to overarching performance objectives.

Boosting Adoption Through Custom Tools

Even with strong strategy and operations, sales execution depends on frontline reps skillfully conducting high-value activities. Unfortunately, rigid out-of-the-box CRM functionality often hinders field productivity.

Here, customization means identifying impediments to sales execution based on rep feedback, then configuring tailored tools and real-time data access to address pain points. Examples include in-app guided selling templates, automated field activity capture from mobile, and context-aware knowledge article recommendations based on opportunity details.

With frictionless access to customer intelligence needed to progress deals, integrated directly into existing workflows, user adoption excels. Empowered sales teams who can work seamlessly ultimately drive more pipeline through customized CRM tools purpose-built around their selling needs.

Informing Decisions Through Reporting

As a sales leader, real-time visibility into performance metrics aligned to strategic KPIs is essential for understanding what's working and adjusting appropriately. This is where customized analytics, dashboards and embedded reporting reveal their value.

For example, executive dashboards could feature targeted lead conversion rates, sales cycle or quota attainment percentages to gauge operational health. Manager dashboards may display team attainment of revenue forecasts to identify coaching needs. Rep dashboards could show individuals' attainment and activity metrics versus peers.

Deeper reporting can uncover additional trends around stage progression, win rates by product line or segment, and pipeline value by source to refine strategy.

This tailored visibility layer translates CRM activity data into strategic insights leaders need to demonstrate performance, fine-tune playbooks, and accelerate sales growth.

With an optimized CRM experience directly informed by your teams' workflows and intelligence needs, reps stay focused on selling, managers have transparency to guide strategy, and executives validate data-driven returns from one unified system.

Chapter Five

CRM and Customer Journey Mapping

C ustomer loyalty is no longer a given for brands. Providing personalized, valuable experiences throughout every touchpoint drives sustained engagement and satisfaction levels that keep buyers coming back. This is where seamlessly integrating customer journey mapping insights into your CRM strategy can steer better business outcomes.

A detailed customer journey map charts the full spectrum of touchpoints shaping your audience's brand perceptions, needs and emotions as they interact with your company across channels and contexts over time. While transaction-based metrics have traditionally defined customer value, the qualitative context provided in journey mapping reveals drivers of satisfaction more predictive of loyalty.

Common steps represented may include early research questions, initial purchase triggers and barriers, post-purchase support needs, repurchase influencers, brand impression risks, and advocacy opportunities. Plotting the full cycle of brand interactions, both human and digital, makes clear where friction points risk relationships while moments of delight may inspire loyalty.

While insightful on its own, the real power of customer journey mapping emerges when integrated with CRM data streams. Overlaying journey stages with metrics around lead quality, deal progression, or churn probability helps you listen more astutely to signals driving customer behaviors. You gain vision into experiences most closely tied to conversions, referrals or losses.

From here, your CRM becomes the steering wheel for realigning processes across sales, marketing and success teams to navigate customers on optimal routes. For cold leads, this may involve content offers nurturing education and trust. For rising-risk renewals, proactive help preempting pain drives retention. Across the landscape, priority waypoints inform campaigns, triggers and incentives via CRM automation.

As you work to evolve customer experiences based on integrated customer journey mapping insights, your CRM provides continuous visibility into whether changes achieve relationship objectives around satisfaction, loyalty and lifetime value.

End-to-end tracking presents conversion rates, NPS or CSAT scores from transactional surveys, referral volumes, expansion revenue, and churn likelihood alerts indicating strategy efficacy across mapped journey segments. Feedback loops help continuously refine waypoint rescue missions and individual treatment based on risk or value tiers.

Over time, the ability to correlate journey stages with bottom-line CRM data uncovers highest-yield opportunities for experience optimization furthering loyalty. The integrated perspectives keep your brand aligned to customer needs even as markets change. With their trusted advisor securing the best route forward, customers follow eagerly at each turn.

The destination for lasting business relationships rests on fully understanding what experiences customers value most. By uncovering those insights through detailed journey mapping integrated with CRM intelligence, you gain the vision and agility to build routes keeping customers returning time and again.

Mapping the Customer Journey

Understanding how customers interact with your business across the entirety of their relationship lifecycle is essential for delivering positive experiences that foster loyalty. Mapping out the customer journey illuminates key stages and touchpoints to optimize based on buyer needs and preferences. While methodologies abound, most effective journey mapping processes share common components. By plotting awareness through advocacy milestones with intelligence-building empathy, gaps become visible that allow tailored messaging and seamless hand-offs between teams. The result is an orchestrated path that accelerates conversion momentum.

Step 1: Plot the Steps Customers Take as Their Relationship Evolves

Every customer relationship evolves through a progression of phases, from initial brand discovery through post-purchase loyalty building. The customer journey map visualizes this evolution at critical process milestones and touchpoints. Touchpoints represent moments of interaction across channels - website visits, information gathering, email opens etc. Milestones mark meaningful transitions between stages.

For example, common high-level journey stages include:

Awareness - Learning of a company, product category or solution to a problem
Consideration - Evaluating if offerings match needs and comparing competitive options
Decision - Selecting a specific product or vendor
Onboarding - Getting set up with purchased solutions for usage
Implementation - Integrating solutions into business processes and workflows
Adoption - Using solutions actively day-to-day after ramp up
Expansion - Growing usage through upsells, cross-sells and upgraded tiers of service

Extension - Continuing usage over years while voicing satisfaction and preferring options

Every industry and product niche will contain variations on this lifecycle theme. Delineating stages, then overlaying supporting processes and associated touchpoints provides a blueprint for optimization. The goal is mapping an ideal progression where customer needs sync with business capabilities at proper times to facilitate growth.

Step 2: Build Journey Personas Based on Common Attributes

Rarely does a singular path define all customers. Instead multiple iterations emerge based on shared attributes and behaviors. Customer personas group users exhibiting similar journeys for analysis. Trends exposed help guide appropriate content, offers and channel targeting for each segment.

For example, potential personas may include:

Direct Buyers - Researched requirements themselves before purchasing through company reps. Move quickly from consideration to purchase once engaged.
Influenced Buyers - Learned about solutions from trade publications, events or peers first before engaging. Longer to develop preference so focus on building awareness and trust.
Solution Buyers - Have very specific existing issues requiring fixes or improvement. Often reach out with targeted questions around capabilities before sharing business contexts.

Each persona aligns messaging and interactions to better fit distinct audience expectations. Persona clustering also informs measurement plans that quantify effectiveness at various process points.

Step 3: Map Current and Future Journeys with Data-Driven Empathy

Effective journey mapping combines quantitative behavioral data with qualitative insights around emotional elements. Metrics expose volumes and conversions between stages while direct customer inputs reveal pain points and moments of delight. Together the Why becomes clearer behind the What and When.

For example, usage data may show a large drop off in active users two months after purchase. User interviews uncover this coincides with implementation frustrations around specific software features. The journey map then targets onboarding improvements to better support feature adoption before falling engagement.

Approaching mapping through the lens of customer experience also builds organizational empathy. Internal teams better understand buyer challenges, questions and perceptions. Quantified metrics benchmark performance at different touchpoints. Customer commentary spotlights areas of misalignment between expectations and realities. The combination informs action plans to exceed expectations by rectifying journey friction points.

Common mapping methods include:

- Surveys gathering structured feedback on processes, emotions and desired improvements

- Focus groups exploring specific steps and interactions in the journey

- Individual interviews probing customer recall across touchpoints

- Analytics leveraging behavioral data systems to quantify volumes and conversions

- Testing through tools tracking on-site movements and engagement

Analytics inform the baselining of efforts while qualitative data brings the journey to life with compounding detail. Together they produce an actionable model for enhancement evaluations.

Optimize Journeys Through the Lens of Buyer Needs

The ultimate goal of mapping is creating superior customer experiences that promote mutually beneficial relationships. By deconstructing current journeys against idealized processes, improvement opportunities become visible across channels, offers and messaging.

The buyer perspective grounds this transformation work in what matters most - their needs at each stage. Stepping mentally into persona shoes, look for misalignments between content served and knowledge sought. Assess eased transitions across touchpoints versus abrupt experience shifts from lack of coordination. Feel the frustration around snags and delays that degrade confidence.

These insights rebuild sequences with the customer placed front and center. Potential optimization paths include:

- Orchestrating hand-offs for integrated messaging across teams

- Crafting stage-specific content that answers persona questions

- Refining processes around known persona pain points

- Automating personalized follow-ups post-purchase

- Seeking regular feedback once implemented

Optimization also elevates areas of existing strength. Strong positive correlations between campaign exposure and sales ready leads informs budget allocation and related performance incentives. Outsized returns from particular segments signals opportunities doubling down on associated experiences.

Continual refinement relies on customer input, whether passive or participatory. Voice of the customer programs institutionalize feedback channels while journey mapping workshops and focus groups provide immersive learning. Together they connect strategy to served experience amidst continually evolving buyer expectations.

Key Elements Make Customer Journey Mapping Impactful

For mapping projects to catalyze real change, they must deliver actionable strategic direction. Common pitfalls leave organizations lost in overcomplexity or devoid of human truth by solely relying formulas. Avoid information overload and ambiguity through these best practices:

- Executives sponsor efforts to instill accountability and ensure adoption

- Cross-functional mapping builds connections between previous silos

- Focus initially on primary persona priorities to establish clarity

- Quantify insights but also capture emotional commentary

- Map both present realities and desired future states

- Link journey stages to specific metrics for performance tracking

- Develop personas beyond demographics to include psychological traits

- Update analysis yearly as changes reshape interactions

With the proper framing, information sources, and participation, maps provide clear direction on improving end-to-end journeys. They align systems, processes and even internal culture to what customers need at each stage while optimizing toward ultimately loyal relationships. Commitments to continual refinement also builds infrastructure sustaining engagement over long-term evolutions in the market.

Leveraging CRM for Improved Customer Experiences

Customer experience defines brand differentiation and loyalty more than ever. How your audience feels during every interaction - across devices, contexts and time - shapes perceptions, satisfaction and lifetime value. This is where a strategic customer relationship management (CRM) strategy becomes critical. By centralizing contextual intelligence and orchestrating personalized engagements, CRM lays the foundation for customer experiences that truly stand out.

Let's explore key mechanisms a holistic CRM approach can activate to shape positive brand impressions and sustain meaningful customer relationships over the long term.

Informing Personalized Interactions

Thanks to internet transparency, today's buyers have high expectations of relevant, frictionless brand experiences and communications tailored to their needs. Mass segmentation no longer suffices. A CRM system's consolidated customer profiles, preferences and engagement data informs the real-time personalization driving perceived value.

For example, email content tailored to past purchase types and website behavior makes outreach resonate better than generic messaging. Support agents accessing order history and past issues can reference specifics for more authentic service. Chatbots can even greet loyalty members by name and make intelligent recommendations based on transaction logs.

Consistently referencing rich CRM insights across these micro-moments shapes the feeling that your brand "gets me" - building emotional affinity through relevance. Over time, AI-driven analytics further help optimize and connect experiences based on engagement patterns, lifetime value tiers and changing interests.

Proactively Mitigating Pain Points

Even with excellent products, occasional issues inevitably affect some customers negatively. However, the brands that demonstrate care through swift response and resolution retain trust despite problems. Here CRM case management, sentiment tracking and triggers enable getting ahead of risks.

For instance, real-time speech analytics could detect rising frustration during customer calls, allowing agents to de-escalate. Analyzing support ticket data can reveal recurring issues to address proactively with users. Transaction logs may reveal drop-offs signaling UX friction for optimization. Taking corrective actions powered by CRM insights leaves customers feeling heard and cared for, rather than abandoned.

Creating Emotional Connections

At its heart, standout customer experience is emotional, tapping universal truths of feeling understood, valued and cared for. CRM data linking interactions to relationship milestones helps nurture powerful connections through celebratory experiences.

For example, thank you messages after first purchases or anniversaries, exclusive loyalty offers for committed customers, or personalized progress updates toward goals all reinforce bonds beyond transactions. Listeners capturing life events even allow support agents to demonstrate genuine empathy. During moments of meaning, CRM-coordinated experiences resonate as authentic because they reflect individual context.

Evaluating and Evolving Journeys

While optimizing known experiences, CRM analytics also fuel constant improvement by revealing influence of broader journey qualities on engagement. Sentiment scores, churn predictors, surveys and correlations of interactions to revenue/referrals quantify where current strategies excel or fall short at holistic relationship-building.

These insights feed iterative experiments enhancing weak journey stages. Creative teams develop journey map scenarios plotting the impact new interventions like workshops, membership perks or events could have on high-risk moments. After rollout, CRM metrics confirm which innovations advance customer priorities best, guiding continual experience enhancement.

With so many factors affecting evolving customer perspectives, only CRM data translates impressions into focused improvements that sustain positive brand affiliations amidst change.

The Differentiation is in the Details

Across industries, brands increasingly realize customer experience is the most sustainable advantage as competition intensifies globally. But generic promises of "putting customers first" no longer persuade savvy audiences judging on evidence.

This is where CRM, as a true experience intelligence hub, becomes the ultimate differentiation engine. Only robust, real-time 360-degree customer insights co-ordinated across all collective brand touchpoints can facilitate the meaningful, consistent and evolving engagement today's buyers expect. When technology and teams work symbiotically to earn relationships through superior under-standing and care, you earn market dominance one customer at a time.

That's the CRM difference.

Chapter Six

Automating Sales Processes

For sales teams, time is the most precious resource. More time allows for more customer interactions and closes more deals. However, the 24-hour day remains fixed. This is where automating repetitive sales tasks through a CRM system comes in - it frees up valuable selling time. This chapter explores the sales productivity benefits of CRM-based automation.

Much of what salespeople do daily are low value, tedious activities like data entry and status reporting. Automation handles these mundane chores, acting as a "digital assistant" to keep the sales workflow running smoothly. This liberates sales reps to spend more time actually selling - interacting with prospects and customers to drive revenue. By incorporating automation, teams can achieve more without sacrificing work-life balance.

There are sales automation tools tailored to every stage of the pipeline. Lead generation can be automated through email campaigns, website visits, and social media. Email follow-ups keep leads warm in between calls. Appointment scheduling, proposal delivery and other sales tasks can also be systematized and streamlined. This end-to-end automation produces a higher volume of leads and a better customer experience.

Leveraging automation, small teams can achieve the sales outcomes only much larger teams could in the past. By handling repetitive chores, even a handful of sales reps can effectively nurture and convert a very large pool of prospects. Like leveraging any technology, automation provides force multiplication for sales efforts leading to greater revenue with the same headcount.

As business aim to cost-effectively increase sales capacity, process automation is essential. While no substitute for human selling skills, automating mundane tasks allows skilled reps to focus on high-value selling activities. Over time, standardized and increasingly efficient workflows compound team productivity. This creates a virtuous cycle propelling sales, customer satisfaction and profits forward.

Boost Sales Productivity with CRM Automation

For resource-constrained sales teams, the only path to growing revenue is working smarter - not harder. This means strategically applying technology to amplify sellers' productivity. Customer relationship management (CRM) systems provide embedded tools to automate repetitive, low value sales tasks. When leveraged fully, these automations act as "digital assistants" freeing up capacity for sellers to focus on high-impact selling activities.

CRM platforms offer end-to-end coverage of the sales process from generating leads all the way through closing deals. Software functionality handles administrative chores in each phase. This leaves sales reps with more bandwidth for actually engaging prospects and nurturing deals. The system becomes a "hybrid" blending automated routines for handling data with a human touch for persuasion and relationship-building.

While no substitute for skilled selling, automations excel at scaling capacity for specific types of repetitive tasks essential to sales operations. When applied judiciously to the right activities, automations multiply productivity. Seven prime functions to consider automating include:

Deal Guidance Automation

Problem: Sales reps juggle many responsibilities across multiple opportunities, making it easy to overlook looming deadlines or drop balls on key tasks. This causes deals to stall unnecessarily.

Solution: CRM automation sets reminders and alerts tuned to each deal's cadence so sellers stay on top of upcoming to-do's before they become issues. Software acts as a personal assistant preventing any slipped responsibilities.

Benefit: More oversight means fewer missed activities. With automations tracking milestones diligently, a higher percentage of opportunities make it successfully across the finish line and convert to revenue.

Lead Management Automation

Problem: Unqualified leads demand time yet seldom convert, wasting precious seller capacity that should be focused on riper prospects.

Solution: Lead scoring algorithms automatically rate incoming leads based on characteristics like recency, frequency, past purchases, title, etc. Software then assigns higher scoring leads to reps as priorities.

Benefit: By preventing sellers from squandering effort on unqualified leads, their time gets redirected to warmer prospects that warrant attention and are more likely to convert with some nurturing. This efficiency multiplies conversion rates.

Communication Automation

Problem: Modern buyers expect rapid responses yet sales reps cannot scale communication capacity infinitely. Critical inquiries get missed or answered late, impairing customer satisfaction.

Solution: Chatbots and email automations handle common questions around the clock, enabling some coverage during off-hours or when personnel occupied. Customers feel supported 24/7.

Benefit: Increased responsiveness and higher customer satisfaction even when rep capacity capped. Systems gather context for complex follow-ups saving human effort.

Data Entry Automation

Problem: Manual data entry like updating customer records or opportunity details is repetitive and consumes too much seller time that could be spent on revenue-generating activities.

Solution: Systems pre-populate fields by pulling from available databases so reps need only make minor tweaks rather than fully manually entering records. Updates require fewer clicks.

Benefit: Automating these mundane tasks significantly reduces the daily administrative burden on sellers. The hours of capacity regained yearly gets reallocated to more strategic seller activities.

Record Creation Automation

Problem: Manually documenting every sales interaction, website visitor and early-stage prospect is vital yet extremely labor intensive, often getting deprioritized by reps focused on servicing existing deals.

Solution: Systems automatically log details like contacts, companies and early buying signals as they occur, effortlessly populating CRM with new records.

Benefit: Reps freed from data entry can better focus on high-touch selling while system captures every signal - enabling future prioritization. Sales and marketing gain fuller visibility into the early funnel.

Research Automation

Problem: Identifying net-new accounts that warrant sales outreach requires extensive manual research across disparate sources - a massively tedious effort yielding mixed results.

Solution: Automated research algorithms mine multiple public and proprietary data sources using defined ideal customer criteria to surface targeted, high-potential prospects. Curated lead lists get routed to CRM and assigned to reps.

Benefit: Software aptly handles the grunt work of discovery freeing up seller capacity while uncovering more needle-in-haystack prospects. The resulting new pipeline opportunities drive greater revenue growth.

Activity Logging Automation

Problem: Tracking interactions across open opportunities to assess where each stands, what's next and when to follow up is incredibly tedious manual work, often deprioritized by reps focused on selling. Yet without logging no pipeline visibility.

Solution: Systems automatically document emails, calls, meetings related to specific opportunities for accurate ongoing progress tracking without any seller effort.

Benefit: Real-time visibility into activity levels and deal advancement without requiring painful manual logging. Data also feeds forecasts and analytics.

Scheduling Automation

Problem: Coordinating meetings relies on tedious back-and-forth email exchanges while sales reps juggle many other obligations. This friction slows deal progress and strains customer experience.

Solution: Scheduling automation allows prospects self-service access to instantly view rep availability and directly book appointments online. Systems sync updates across users and tools.

Benefit: Convenience and control for customers combined with major time savings for sellers make appoint booking seamless at scale without compromising relationships for efficiency.

Personalized Email Automation

Problem: Buyers expect tailored messaging yet basic email marketing feels impersonal. Crafting individual emails manually doesn't scale while blasting the same generic messages alienates recipients.

Solution: Automated triggerstied to prospect behaviors/attributes enable sending personalized content at scale. Messages feel customized with contextual references and relevant offers for each recipient.

Benefit: Combined scalability and personalization achieve the best of both worlds. Tailored interactions drive higher engagement, response rates, and ultimately revenue.

Optimized Prospecting Automation

Problem: Finding net-new potential customers amidst growing data volumes feels like an endless and aimless task. Most leads sourced prove low quality, wasting crucial selling time.

Solution: Prospecting automation mines sources using custom criteria, scoring results to uncover hidden gems. Software routes hyper-targeted, high-propensity leads into CRM assigning them to appropriate reps.

Benefit: Letting algorithms handle discovery and prioritization based on ideal customer profiles makes the best use of technology. Reps freed from grunt work then convert referred leads more efficiently.

Automated Reporting

Problem: Centralized reports often provide broad overviews when users need specific real-time cuts on metrics like their performance, territory, product line, etc. Yet customizing views manually demands extensive, ongoing effort.

Solution: Automation systems instantly prepare customized reports for each user based on their role. Management, marketing and reps all get the exact business intel they need, when they need it, without creating or deciphering anything manually.

Benefit: Automated reporting tailored to each audience alleviates the pains of manual analysis while empowering smarter decisions through readily available insights. This drives strategy, optimization and growth.

Call List Automation

Problem: Business development demands maximizing conversations to drive opportunities yet manual dialing consumes extensive time between calls. Days fill with downtime instead of dialog.

Solution: Auto-dialers streamline call lists by automatically phasing contacts while also recording details for future reference. Systems minimize idle time between calls to keep reps constantly engaged.

Benefit: Putting machines to work maximizing connections frees up seller capacity. Increased conversations and reduced overhead drives more opportunities in the pipeline.

Chatbot Conversational Automation

Problem: Buyers expect instant responses yet human capacity for handling inquiries caps out. Sellers end up overlooking key questions and customers feel ignored without 24/7 support.

Solution: Chatbots provide conversational interactions, answering common questions around the clock with voice and language tailored to match service reps. Bots handle easy inquiries while gathering context on complex issues for later follow-up.

Benefit: Increased responsiveness coupled with greater customer satisfaction through anytime coverage and handoffs to subject matter experts. Chatbots ultimately become trusted advisors.

Forecasting Automation

Problem: Predicting future sales based on past trends and current pipeline requires extensively analyzing disparate sets of dense historical data - a massively manual effort yielding limited insights.

Solution: Purpose-built forecasting tools automatically compile and assess real-time data to generate projections for any date range and category. Systems account for trends, seasonality, rep performance and more when modeling.

Benefit: Automated forecasting provides instant visibility into expected results empowering smarter resource allocation and performance optimization without manual number crunching.

Proposal/Document Automation

Problem: Collating opportunities then manually customizing quotes, contracts, collateral like capability briefings is an intensive, repetitive effort that doesn't scale. Yet generic content falls flat.

Solution: Document automation systems integrate with CRM data to auto-populate and tailor templated proposals, slides and other sales material to each prospect's unique situation with a few clicks.

Benefit: Automated document creation eliminates grunt work while still allowing customization and personalization that captures deals. This blending of scalability and relevance drives higher proposal-to-close rates.

CRM Analytics Automation

Problem: Key patterns and trends hide within CRM data that could optimize strategy and performance if uncovered. But managers lack the bandwidth to continually analyze datasets manually searching for signals.

Solution: Embedded analytics highlight correlations, customer behaviors, win/loss commonalities and more to provide insights without requiring dedicated data science resources. Systems surface recommendations.

Benefit: Automated analytics alleviate the need for manual assessment while still powering strategic discoveries that can transform sales, marketing and service approaches to drive greater growth.

Territory/Quota Automation

Problem: Mapping geographic sales regions and allocating customer assignments involves assessing many complex variables. Likewise calibrating quotas and capacity models requires predictive acumen most leaders lack. Suboptimal mappings and targets result.

Solution: Algorithms scientifically balance workloads, headcount and potential across regions based on historicals and modeling. Systems determine optimal market and quota distributions based on data.

Benefit: Automated territory and quota calculations precisely calibrate workloads, capacity and potential boosting motivation along with results. Companies sell smarter through technology-enabled decisions.

Pricing Automation

Problem: Defining pricing thresholds is challenging amidst shifting market conditions, customer willingness-to-pay and competitors. Relying on intuition leaves money on the table. Yet assessing signals manually overwhelms.

Solution: Usage metrics, transaction data, surveys and benchmarks feed automated pricing tools that define and update optimal price points for each product, region and customer tier.

Benefit: Algorithmic price optimization maximizes yield by scientifically aligning pricing to value delivery, demand signals, costs and position - driving higher margins.

Getting Started with Sales Automation

Implementing automation is a gradual, phased journey rather than an overnight overhaul. Begin by methodically identifying the most painful friction points where your team currently gets bogged down in manual work. Common bottlenecks include:

- Repeatedly having to manually enter customer data into systems

- Struggling to keep track of next steps across a large volume of open deals

- Missing sales tasks and activities due to forgotten responsibilities

- Difficulty responding to customer inquiries in a timely fashion

- An inability to promptly follow up with every lead due to high volume

- No visibility into individual rep performance and pipeline projections

Pinpoint exactly where excessively manual processes are hindering sales velocity, capacity and productivity. Then explore where software automation functionality could alleviate these root causes.

Prioritize attacking the areas that will have the biggest return on investment first. Some good candidates to start with often include automating data entry, logging activities, and assigning tasks and reminders. Software can instantly lift these burdens from reps' shoulders so they can focus energy on higher-level selling work.

Early on, limit the number of automations implemented concurrently so the team isn't overwhelmed by software tools. As your sales organization gets comfortable leveraging the initial tools, progressively layer on additional automations at a measured pace. With each new capability brought online, provide ample training and information to users on how the automation works and the benefits it drives.

Over a period of several quarters, systematically build up a customized automation toolkit addressing your most critical sales friction areas. Treat these tools as digital assistants, not as replacing your skilled sales reps but as force multipliers that create leverage and lift productivity.

As the technology permeates processes, revisit your sales workflows periodically and continue to refine them. Look for ways to tweak handoff points between manual and automated work to further optimize efficiency. Expect to continually make minor enhancements even as the broad automation framework remains consistent.

Implementing sales automation is not just a technology initiative but rather an organizational change effort. Without proper change management, tools fail to get embraced and transform ways of selling. Follow these 8 key steps to ensure user buy-in across roles that maximizes automation ROI:

Secure Executive Endorsement

Gaining leadership's public backing is mission-critical so the shift cascades deliberately across the business, not bottoms-up. When C-suite champions automation, allocating resources and broadcasting goals, it signals organizational priority. Managers in turn fully engage in the transition knowing expectations come from above. Reps also take note and view adoption as advancing their careers rather than optional. Top-down sponsorship is essential.

Incentivize Sales Management Leading Change

Frontline sales managers directly interface with reps daily, influencing opinions and behaviors significantly. Unless they wholeheartedly support automation, usage will lag. Providing incentives for sales leaders hitting targets for usage metrics encourages their championing change. When managers coach teams on navigating workflows or showcase automation benefits, tools get leveraged. Rewarding those stewarding adoption guarantees their commitment.

Spotlight Benefits Addressing End-User Frictions

The only way to convince sales reps to alter their daily routines reliance on new tools is showing how automation directly alleviates their pains. Reduce the emphasis on big-picture productivity gains for the company. Instead, highlight benefits addressing rep frustrations like eliminating manual data entry or automatically logging activities they normally avoid. Better proposals with fewer clicks resonate. If automation makes their lives easier, adoption emerges bottom-up even without mandates.

Install Measurement Systems Tied to Goals

Automation outcomes do not materialize automatically but rather require concerted efforts driven by goals. Establish specific targets for usage, efficiency and revenue growth with clocks tracking progress. Creating healthy urgency fuels teams to realize benefits. Especially early on, measure adoption levels and individual contributions. As execs review metrics frequently, managers rally their reports around hitting key automation milestones that factor into reviews.

Allocate Ongoing Training Resources

While some intuitively adopt automation, others require extensive handholding that builds skills gradually through repetition. Budgeting adequate resources for side-by-side training and long-term skills development is imperative, especially with frequent software enhancements. Always have internal experts accessible who can walk reps through new features while addressing questions. Sustained learning opportunities remove barriers as teams expand their automation acumen over 24 months until leveraging tools is second nature.

Incentivize Tech-Savvy Peer Advocates

Every sales unit has reps more readily embracing change and innovation. Identify these "automation advocates" passionate about elevating performance through technology and leverage them. Allow pilot groups to test tools and share peer experiences that often resonate more than expert directives. Even incentivize top adopters to coach peers still reluctant to automate workflows initially. Once advocates model benefits in action, belief follows.

Publicize Early Automation Wins

Even small early successes using automation build confidence in systems across teams, spurring further usage. Quantify efficiency gains around saved hours or meetings booked that couldn't be done manually at scale. Celebrate incremental improvements automation enabled from optimized prospecting to expanded email outreach. Publicize examples where technology increased output without substantially growing headcount. Soon groups compete to achieve standout results leveraging tools.

Collect Feedback to Refine Functionality

Flawless automation adoption from the outset is exceedingly rare. Expect to uncover workflow holes or new user requests once reps operate tools under real workplace pressures and contexts not considered initially by technologists. Setup channels soliciting user feedback on enhancements that would facilitate usage or improve experiences. Show teams their input spurs real improvements wins over skeptics. By the 2nd or 3rd update addressing feedback, reluctance fades.

The Way Forward for Sales Leaders

For ambitious companies aiming to scale revenue without proportionately growing headcount, sales automation is mandatory. Handled delicately, software can alleviate sellers' tedium while increasing the velocity and efficiency of pipeline throughput. This establishes a positive spiral where small, empowered teams produce exponentially greater results through technology-enabled leverage - the ultimate competitive edge.

Rather than viewing automation as threatening to replace staff, embrace it as augmenting the productivity of your selling professionals. When tactfully introduced and championed by leaders, users will adopt these force-multiplying tools that liberate them from drudgery. Over 24 months, aim for a scenario where reps rely upon and leverage automation assistants daily. Gradually these technologies transform operations as they are embedded into standard workflows.

With the time and energy freed up, redirect your selling talent to the points of greatest customer impact and upside. Orient reps toward consultative relationship-building, complex solution design, strategic value communication and negotiation. Develop broader solution expertise through training. While management drudgery recedes automated into the background, let your empowered sellers form trusted advisor partnerships that compel clients to grow wallet share.

This human+machine approach represents the future of selling - with administrative tasks disappearing into AI, while the human touch remains indispensable. As a leader, actively shepherd your team toward this more rewarding model leveraging smart application of technology.

Chapter Seven

Enhancing Sales Communication

C lear and consistent communication lies at the core of sales success. When sales teams are able to effectively communicate with key customer contacts, relationships thrive. This leads to increased sales, repeat business, valuable referrals and expanded opportunities.

However, communication breakdowns rapidly diminish sales performance. Misunderstandings frustrate clients and breed dissatisfaction. Lack of coordination across sales, service and support functions presents an incoherent image that erodes trust. Before long, hard-won accounts begin to crumble.

That's why implementing a customer relationship management (CRM) platform is critical for sales-driven organizations. By coordinating customer communication across departments, CRM systems enable teams to present a unified face to valuable accounts. This establishes the open, responsive and reliable communication channels that customers demand.

The Power of CRM-Driven Follow-Up in Sales

In sales, diligently tending to client needs is essential for retention and growth. With packed schedules managing multiple active leads and accounts, following up promptly can become an afterthought. But inconsistent or missing follow-up frustrates clients and erodes trust in your capabilities.

That's why implementing follow-up discipline through CRM systems offers transformative potential for sustaining client relationships. By automating next step tasks based on campaign interactions, CRM tools promote accountability around quick, organized and reliable follow-up.

The Power of Triggered Follow-Up

CRM platforms unlock smarter follow-up through triggered actions tied to multi-channel campaign components. For example, sending a targeted email newsletter provides visibility into who opens, clicks or downloads from that mailing. CRM can automatically log tasks pushing immediate outreach to engaged recipients.

By triggering direct follow-up to campaign responders, sales teams capitalize on rising interest signals. Prompt outreach reinforces relevancy, answers questions and advances opportunities while interest runs high. Avoiding lags between demonstrated interest and sales contact optimizes lead nurturing momentum.

Applied more broadly across campaigns spanning email, social media, events and content offers, triggered follow-up tasks enable hyper-responsive engagement. Lead scoring models can determine sales-ready thresholds based on cumulative campaign interactions, automatically notifying reps to pursue hot opportunities.

Eliminating Follow-Up Gaps

Beyond manual outreach oversights, team coordination gaps also delay follow-up around shared accounts. Transitioning leads from marketing to sales often creates response lags, with both teams assuming the other will make contact. Further hand-offs to account managers can perpetuate delays across the client lifecycle.

CRM systems consolidate insights to eliminate interdepartmental swivel chair scenarios. Shared activity histories provide follower context and next step clarity regardless of contributing team. Role-based views ensure relevant stakeholders get notified upon lead transfers or new interactions. Tighter coordination around accounts through CRM enhances follow-up velocity across organizations.

Getting ahead of lead falloff rates requires establishing reliable CRM-powered follow-up protocols. Best practices include:

- Configure triggered actions from campaigns and account changes to automatically log next task steps

- Set SLA policies for initial and ongoing follow-up cadences based on lead scores

- Notify cross-functional teams upon lead hand-offs to align around ownership

- Review reports on aging or incomplete tasks to ensure accountability

While no system can replace human judgment around lead prioritization and messaging, CRM-driven process rigor can prevent promising opportunities from slipping through the cracks. Establishing follow-up accountability through automated notifications and escalations helps sales teams deliver on the promise of responsive care.

Follow-up consistency makes the difference between frustrated one-time clients and delighted lifelong customers. With CRM improving oversight into who needs what next, sales organizations can nurture leads with the prompt attention that builds revenues and referrals.

Driving Key Account Success through CRM Communication

In the quest to gain greater wallet share and loyalty from key accounts, communication sits at the crux of success or failure. Lucrative enterprise deals and lasting B2B relationships alike depend on maintaining open, responsive and trust-based interactions across complex buying committees.

Yet as account coverage expands across sales territories and verticals, communication coordination frequently falters:

- Mixed messages confuse and frustrate key contacts

- Information gaps result in disjointed, uninformed responses

- Poor hand-offs leave valuable communications unanswered

- Competing outreach from field reps overwhelms recipients

- Hard-won opportunities stall without prompt issue resolution

Amidst the chaos of multifaceted sales communication, even strong relationships run off the rails. CRM systems offer account teams a way to meet soaring communication demands through organizational alignment.

CRM Communication Infrastructure for Key Accounts

At its core, CRM software provides the scaffolding for orchestrating and optimizing customer communication across sales organizations. Features like shared contact profiles, activity logging and automated notifications give account team members visibility to better coordinate messaging and responses.

This transforms fragmented, personality-driven exchanges into a more cohesive brand experience aligned around account needs. By strengthening communication continuity through CRM:

- Sales, service and support staff access shared context to deliver consistent, personalized responses

- Executive sponsors and subject matter experts loop into conversations to resolve issues quickly

- Account history visibility prevents repetitive inquiries and guides next actions

- Contact insights inform tailored messaging and media for enhanced relevance

- Automated workflows eliminate response gaps from hand-offs or ownership changes

As communication flows more freely across internal teams, customer satisfaction inevitably rises. More responsive and coordinated exchanges demonstrate credible capabilities that inspire trust in your guidance. Issues dissipate, projects progress and new opportunities emerge when messaging resonates.

Optimizing Targeted Communication Relevance

But CRM systems allow sales teams to further optimize external communication through targeted, segmented outreach. While mass emails or events may reach broad audiences, personalized messaging drives relevance.

Contact profiling tools capture role, industry, past purchases and area data to micro-target content. Contextualized outreach demonstrates you understand key contacts' unique needs and challenges. This relevance captures attention amidst inbox noise.

Behavioral tracking in CRM also fuels insight to align follow-on communication with demonstrated interests. As key contacts engage with campaigns, activity logging tools note content downloads, site pageviews, email clicks and event participation. Customer boards display aggregate activity to guide next talking points.

In this sense, CRM serves as an external communication optimization engine. Tightly interlinked profiling, tracking and automation features help sales teams hyper-personalize messaging for relevance. This captures share of mind and share of wallet with indispensable, highly anticipated account communications.

With CRM providing underlying infrastructure to smooth and enhance external communication, sales leaders must guide effective adoption across account teams. Key steps include:

1. *Establish accurate contact profiles* - Comprehensive records of core buying committee members provide the customer insights for tailoring communication. Capture details spanning roles, goals, pain points, and communication behaviors/preferences to inform follow-on exchanges. Maintain clear segmentations across contacts based on their influence levels and focus areas from technical reviewers to executive sponsors. Supplement with social profiles and contextual research for deeper backgrounds.

2. *Log all interactions* - Making notes on every meaningful customer touchpoint, no matter how small, creates vital context for eliminating repetitive inquiries. Activity logging provides timelines of sent proposals, delivered on-site presentations, responses to functionality questions, and agreed project milestones. Tie documented commitments directly to corporate or contact records for easy reference and tracking. Sync logged notes across account leadership for universal visibility. Upload related file shares and recordings as communication artifacts linked to discussions.

3. *Set automated alerts and workflows* - With interaction details stored centrally in the CRM system, configure targeted alerts for critical notifications across team members. Trigger email notifications automatically based on key events such as requested proposal delivery dates or project approval delays. Assign and route subsequent response tasks instantly to maintain momentum. Use automated hand-offs and

introductions to align expanding account contacts with relevant new sales resources equipped to provide specialized counsel. Minimize gaps through rapid conflict identification, issue escalation and resource reallocation using system workflows.

4. *Motivate usage discipline* - Given the scale of account-wide communications, CRM adoption requires deliberate reinforcement and accountability. Leading with senior management buy-in signals importance for diligent system utilization. Provide individual user scorecards benchmarking activity logging and communication responsiveness versus goals. Call out gaps relative to high performers. Share success stories and client testimonials for teams demonstrating communication excellence powered by CRM. Incorporate performance into sales compensation reviews and leadership development discussions to motivate continuous improvement.

5. *Analyze contact analytics* - Detailed activity history tracking in the CRM system provides a goldmine of customer engagement analytics to perfect targeted communication. Profile online content consumption behaviors across websites, emails, and product collateral to determine topics of greatest interest by role. Refine industry-specific messaging for enhanced relevance. Track offer acceptance and referrals to define communication contribution and influence levels of each contact. Continually tailor follow-up talking points based on prior interactions and demonstrated preferences for a better return on communication efforts.

While no technology can replace the skill of building rapport across C-suite relationships, CRM facilitates surrounding external communication. Shared insights, transparent activity and automated orchestration give sales teams advantages in delivering the timely, tailored multichannel experiences that key accounts now expect. When powered by CRM, external sales communication becomes a synchronized competitive edge.

Optimizing Internal Sales Communication

In the race to drive deals and quarterly performance, sales teams often lose sight of overarching strategic priorities. Contacts receive competing, disjointed outreach from reps focused solely on advancing their own pipelines. This breeds customer distrust and deal losses over time from fractured account management.

That's why implementing tighter sales team communication practices is pivotal for sustained success. By keeping reps aligned on target accounts, coordinated around strategies and transparent around activities, organizations present a unified brand voice that earns long-term customer confidence.

This is where collaborative CRM comes in - providing the information architecture for shared customer insights, synchronized calendars and cross-functional engagement feeds. When Harnessing this expanded toolkit, sales managers reign in the bedlam through:

Strategic Territory Planning

- Plot named accounts and contacts on shareable maps

- Define geographic and vertical coverage rules

- Allocate relationships across reps

- Restrict access beyond assigned areas

Activity & Pipeline Visibility

- Maintain open logs of emails, meetings and milestone events

- Monitor individual and team performance metrics

- Surface red flags around stagnating opportunities

- Celebrate and learn from wins

Specialist Coordination

- Tag accounts requiring expert resources

- Automatically loop in solutions engineers

- Introduce executive sponsors where needed

- Align talking points around technical qualifications

These collaborative elements prevent disjointed, maverick selling by enabling transparency, context and oversight into the health of key accounts. But achieving the full potential of collaborative CRM requires motivating consistent adoption across sales teams through:

Leadership Endorsement

- Executives visibly model logging, monitoring and coordinating in the system

- Middle managers echo commitment to transparency expectations

Peer Accountability

- Review participation levels in team meetings

- Recognize top adopters publicly

- Construct peer audits for activity logging

Gamification

- Establish individual user scorecards for utilization

- Reward high performers with choice territories

- Create competitions for adoption metrics

When collaboration behaviors permeate sales culture, the entire organization bands together to present customers the experience promised in marketing messaging - responsive, informed and customer-focused.

Core Elements of a Collaborative CRM Platform

Here are some components in a collaborative CRM. These include interaction management and channel management.

Enabling Streamlined Cross-Team Communication

An expanding array of customer relationship management (CRM) solutions promise sales, marketing and service teams a singular view of customer interactions. But as departments pile disjointed data into generic CRM repositories, consolidation alone proves insufficient for powering genuine collaboration.

True collaborative CRM platforms go further by integrating communication-focused components for aligning insights, interactions and infrastructure across the customer experience:

Interaction Management

The foundation for cross-team transparency, interaction management captures details associated with customer exchanges across departments. Logging calls, emails, chats and in-person meetings in a shared CRM system allows staff to familiarize with past discussions before engaging to ensure continuity.

By documenting customer communication in one place, teams minimize frustrating repeat inquiries and benefit from insight into preferable contact methods for nurturing each account. Sales reps pitch opportunities with fuller context while service agents resolve technical issues armed with order specifics. Access to collective interaction histories coordinates informed, personalized outreach.

Channel Management

But detailed interaction logging is only half the equation. The effectiveness of recorded communications hinges on actively optimizing supporting channels. Do reps struggle connecting with key prospects by phone? Complex e-commerce forms generate frequent customer questions? Channel management addresses such engagement barriers.

Collaborative CRM platforms link communication analytics to existing organizational systems to target weak points. Customer service call volume data could inform hiring additional contact center staff. Negative social media mentions highlight self-service portal UX issues for the web team. Channel management converts observed interaction pain points into action by assigning tasks to responsible owners.

Together, interaction management and channel management transform scattered customer information into improved experiences. Contextualized history-informed discussions occur over appropriately resourced channels, demonstrating customer-centric commitment.

Achieving True Team Alignment

But harvesting the collaboration promise of enterprise CRM requires more than robust tracking and infrastructure capabilities. Streamlining access to insights is only the starting point - leadership must champion transparent communication rituals that permeate team habits.

- Encourage regular peer shadowing for insight exposure

- Celebrate examples of information sharing that averted account crises

- Run interdepartmental working sessions on shared priorities

- Incentivize proactive contributions of intelligence into CRM

With a reinforced culture of openness, sales, marketing and service adopt CRM's collaborative affordances more actively. Teams align around known contacts less as names on a screen but holistic individuals with unique needs.

Real collaboration emerges organically by learning together beyond basics logged in the system.

While no application generates collaboration outright, purpose-built CRM capabilities lay the technical groundwork for radically transparent team alignment. Paired with cultural cues from leadership encouraging increased engagement, cross-functional understanding flourishes.

The Path to Strategic Key Account Communication

Sales organizations must deliver timely, relevant and consistent exchanges across complex buying committees to remain indispensable trusted advisors.

Yet as account coverage expands globally, communication coordination frequently falters:

- Mixed messages confuse C-level contacts

- Disjointed responses erode hard-won trust

- Delayed issue resolution puts deals and renewals at risk

- Disorganized outreach overwhelms recipients

Amidst the chaos, even long-term loyalty waferers. That's why achieving communication mastery must sit atop the sales agenda for any account-driven organization.

CRM systems help sales leaders meet intensifying demands by providing infrastructure for organizing account communication. Features like shared customer profiles, activity logging and engagement analytics enable coordination while still allowing personalization.

This transforms fragmented, personality-driven exchanges into cohesive brand experiences aligned around account needs and buying stage priorities. Tighter communication continuity through CRM:

- Creates informed responses with access to shared context

- Resolves issues quickly by looping appropriate experts

- Prevents repetitive inquiries by exposing full histories

- Informs better tailored outreach based on demonstrated interests

- Eliminates unanswered exchanges through automated workflows

The result is proactive communication that conveys credible capabilities and commitment. As outreach resonates across accounts, satisfaction rises alongside sales. But CRM software alone cannot generate sales communication excellence without adoption fidelity.

The following guideposts should direct the communications:

Secure Executive Sponsorship

Gaining organization-wide adoption for diligent CRM usage starts from the top. When leadership preaches the gospel of communication transparency, contributors recognize the importance of rallying behind platform protocols.

Let data-driven executives and account management sponsors model documentation discipline during internal meetings. Publicly log action items, share insights from recent VIP meetings, and project activity feeds during sessions. Verbally emphasize reliance on CRM for preparing, coordinating and optimizing high-level outreach.

Further motivate adoption through executives reviewing reporting for activity gaps, calling out delinquent teams and defining accountability policies like utilization-based bonuses or consequences. This managerial pressure ensures universal data contribution quality and rates. Promoted from above, the priority of accurate centralized relationship records becomes an unavoidable aspect of sales life.

Launch Targeted Training

With executive emphasis fueling acknowledgement of CRM's crucial role, targeted training initiatives activate adoption by spotlighting practical uses tailored to sales, service and support communication workflows. Avoid broad overviews describing platform capabilities most will rarely leverage. Instead, deliver focused sessions catering to departmental pain points:

Equip market-facing reps to log activity for deal insight sharing, tag technical requirements for specialist loops and configure contact-based workflows to automate introductions upon role changes. Enable service teams with tools for documenting support issues, triggering assistance from experts based on case complexity thresholds and assigning hand-offs to guide customers seamlessly.

Contextualized training centered on role-relevant application drives home direct benefits, breaking barriers to consistent utilization faster. Sustain momentum with supplemental microlearning content drawing CRM best practices from account management case studies.

Monitor Adoption Habits

Despite quality rollout messaging and focused training, leaders must track actual system usage habits to confirm communication coordination permeates CRM-enabled processes.

Identify adoption gaps through activity audit reports indicating thin individual contribution rates. Review contact profile completeness for light fields signaling flawed discipline. Follow-up through one-on-one reviews for understanding roadblocks whether from convoluted interfaces or lack of direct business linkage understanding. Employ light gamification nudges through peer leaderboards celebrating usage rates.

Proactively listening for excuses around manual processes or siloed legacy tools provides opportunities for leadership to realign perspectives. Drive home the customer experience dangers from communication gaps and how CRM mitigates data disconnects.

Reinforce Through Reviews

CRM mastery relies on motivated continuous adoption, not hitting one-time training compliance. Weaving platform utilization and transparent communication directly into professional development conversations and reviews sustains excellence through intrinsic desire for stellar assessments.

Managers should analyze activity logging rates and shared logs as inputs for scoring communication coordination. Does rep outreach reflect coordination with shared team insights? Do service notes demonstrate information sharing that averted escalations? Are strategy adjustments and account warnings visible to all?

Call out gaps relative to benchmarks while spotlighting and rewarding standout cross-team collaborators. Let CRM adoption quality and commitment drive leadership potential diagnoses and compensation outcomes. Raise the consistency bar gradually each review cycle to motivate increasing mastery.

While no technology fosters innate skills like listening and rapport-building, CRM facilitates surrounding coordination. Shared insights and structured processes give sales teams advantages in delivering the calibrated, trust-building communication experiences modern key accounts expect.

Chapter Eight

Managing the Lead-to-Customer Journey

An effective lead management strategy is essential for guiding prospects from initial inquiry through to conversion and beyond. This process involves carefully tracking and nurturing leads, qualifying their potential, and seamlessly progressing them along the sales funnel towards becoming customers. When done right, it leads to higher conversion rates, greater customer lifetime value, and reduced churn.

In this chapter, we will explore best practices around implementing a CRM system to facilitate robust lead management. A properly utilized CRM centralizes all prospect interactions in one place, provides visibility into lead status and health, and enables timely, relevant communication. Together, disciplined processes and the right technology can transform lead management from a chaotic scramble into a smooth, efficient machine.

Capturing and Qualifying Leads with CRM

The customer journey typically begins with an initial lead capture when a prospect first makes contact expressing potential interest. However, not every inquiry will represent a qualified sales opportunity. The ability to efficiently assess lead potential early on and keep track of relevant details is critical to sales success.

This is where a robust CRM system earns its keep by using its functionality to support smooth lead intake, evaluation, tagging, distribution and tracking. When leveraged effectively, these tools qualify sales-ready leads faster, retain better data, coordinate follow-up, and accelerate opportunity conversion. Altogether they generate greater pipeline yield from inbound lead generation efforts.

To further understand why using CRM software is best for lead management, let's look at each step of the traditional process and see how CRM plays into each stage.

Stage 1. Lead Capture

The lead capture process kicks off the sales cycle by registering initial prospect contact and interest. CRM lays the data foundation for downstream lead management by automatically logging inquiries, distributing new contacts, and tracking engagement. When leveraged properly, it makes intake seamless while giving sales operations real-time visibility.

Website chatbots, online forms and call center numbers all channel raw lead data into CRM intake workflows. New contacts get added directly to the centralized database with key details like source, date/time, product interest and basic qualifiers. No manual data entry means faster speed from inquiry to initial outreach.

Once logged, intelligent lead distribution tools assign new contacts to appropriate account owners according to territory, product line, or specialty. Context from past account history and interactions guides matching so conversations continue seamlessly. No time is wasted determining who should pursue which leads.

As leads progress to marketing qualified or even sales qualified status, the CRM automatically compiles a rolling feed of all communications, internal notes and milestone events associated with the record. This visibility assists handoffs between teams while mapping the customer journey over time. The lead's profile essentially tells an always up-to-date story.

With these core capabilities, CRM transforms lead capture from a hit-or-miss scramble to methodical order. Overall intake volume, efficiency and data integrity rise dramatically. For sales operations, better first contact experiences bolster brand impressions while more qualified opportunities enter the pipeline faster.

Stage 2. Lead Enrichment and Tracking

As leads enter the sales pipeline, sizeable info gaps often exist around company details, buying authority, and current solutions. Lead enrichment leverages integration with business data sources to flesh out missing details at scale. Meanwhile, tracking tools compile prospect engagement data to reveal preferences. CRM delivers both enhanced intelligence and a comprehensive audit trail.

To move contacts from anonymous inquiries to fully-profiled opportunities, CRMs connect natively with specialized data enrichment providers. These tap into vast business directories to populate empty fields in the record with employee hierarchies, technologies used, corporate family trees and more. Such context aids initial outreach and shapes sales positioning.

Beyond enriching data, CRM also aggregates activity from the contact record itself - website visits, email opens, event sign-ups, content downloads and similar engagement. This reveals behaviors over time so sales and marketing can better align messaging. Seasonality, trends and spikes inform campaigns and forecasts. A holistic view of customers emerges.

The cumulative impact of captured interactions, dynamically enriched attributes and engagement analytics is a continuously updated lead profile narrative. Like a timeline documenting the relationship stages from stranger to trusted advisor, this equips account teams to reference key moments, past discussions, and upcoming milestones to personalize sales experiences.

With holistic intelligence gathering and centralized tracking, CRM transforms fragmented lead data into strategic advantage. Sales operations avails itself of enhanced lead profiles and activity analysis in service of higher conversion rates.

Stage 3. Assigning Leads and Monitoring Progress

As inbound inquiries roll in, sales operations managers must rapidly distribute leads to account executives according to territory, specialty, capacity, or other parameters. Within the CRM, these assignments should be visible to all relevant stakeholders. Account executives can then begin qualifying lead potential through discovery calls, demos, and other touchpoints.

Here's where lead management can get tricky. Certain events can trigger an overwhelming influx of new leads. CRM software can help you tend to this increase in leads. You can use the software to set criteria that automatically pairs new leads with appropriate sales reps. This way, you'll have an immediate strategy for getting leads to the team member best suited to move them through your sales pipeline. You'll also save the time of speaking with your team to determine who can take which new leads.

CRM lead distribution also enhances your multi-territory sales process. You can set your CRM to designate new leads from a given region to a certain group of sales reps automatically. Your CRM will then choose the right rep from this group based on other criteria. This way, a rep based in your second office isn't working with someone located near your first office, for instance.

The CRM system should capture every interaction in the record for that lead, creating a timeline of engagement. Key details like lead source, contract value, close date, and specific next actions can be tracked as well. With this degree of visibility, managers can monitor lead progress, ensure proper follow-up, and reassign leads if needed. Reports and dashboards provide bird's-eye visibility.

Stage 4. Lead Qualification

Not every lead warrants equal sales attention and resources. The lead qualification process separates hot prospects from more speculative inquiries to ensure pursuit energy aligns with opportunity size. CRM evaluates engagement signals and attributes to automatically categorize leads based on sales-readiness. This allows sales operations to double down where probability of close is highest.

CRM platforms incorporate customizable lead scoring models that assign point values to key behaviors like email opens, content downloads and site visits. Meanwhile, demographic data and firmographic fields also contribute to the score. Higher outputs reflect greater sales potential. Grouping contacts by lead score bands them into hot, warm and cold buckets for tiered follow-up.

Qualification goes beyond just passive scoring though. CRM trigger event-driven workstreams based on score thresholds to prompt account owners. Notifications alert reps when a cold lead turns hot through a flurry of page views. Task reminders ensure nurture sequences launch for newly-warm prospects. And email templates deploy to accelerate hot contacts.

Lead qualification represents a huge data lift for sales operations, analyzing countless attributes and activities to reveal revenue potential. Rather than getting lost in the volume, CRM reporting condenses insights into bird's-eye-view summaries and strips out noise. What factors drive conversions best? Which content resonates most with IT leads versus marketing? The intel guides strategy and optimization.

Stage 5. Scoring and Segmentation

Not all leads represent equal revenue potential. More mature leads that have expressed specific needs and interest are clearly more sales-ready than early stage tire kickers. Lead scoring helps categorize leads based on characteristics that correlate with conversion probability. Common factors include demographics, behaviors like site visits, and qualitative assessments of sales readiness.

Segmenting contacts based on lead score enables account executives to tailor messaging and sales plays. For colder leads, educational nurturing focused on building awareness and interest is appropriate. But for hotter leads actively evaluating solutions, content discussing product specifics and ROI data will resonate more. Aligning outreach to lead segments this way improves results.

Stage 6. Lead Nurturing

In pockets of promising prospect activity hide the seeds of future deals. But with limited sales bandwidth, pursuing every single lead at once dilutes effectiveness. This underscores the value of accurate lead scoring frameworks and thoughtful segmentation within CRM platforms. Together, they route the right leads to the right plays at the right time.

CRM incorporates dynamic lead scoring models to categorize contacts not just by attributes like industry or company size, but also engagement metrics. Values get assigned to key behaviors including email reply rates, content downloads, site visitor frequency/depth and event signups. Meanwhile, firmographic data contributes as well. Added together, the resulting score predicts sales readiness.

By plotting contacts along the numerical score spectrum from low to high, natural breakpoints emerge where clusters of leads share similar conversion potential based on aggregate activity. Applying customized labels like "cold", "warm" and "hot" turns scoring model outputs into segment categories that dictate next actions. No manual sorting needed.

Grouping contacts into targeted segments now means sales operations can craft customized nurture tracks and refine follow-up timing/context without overpersonalizing at scale. Through CRM automation by segment, cold leads receive informative newsletters to build awareness while warm prospects get soft-sell product unveils and hot contacts connect directly with sales for demos.

With these tools, CRM platforms make segment-based selling scalable, preventing leads from stalling out at any point in the process. Strategic categorization, automation and analytics help sales operations double down on prime prospects and aligns resources to opportunity.

Continuous Evaluation and Optimization

An effective lead management process represents a carefully balanced ecosystem where inefficiencies in any part—capture, assignment, qualification, nurturing—reverberate through the whole system. This underscores why regular inspection, assessment and enhancement focused on underperformance underpins sustained sales growth. Fortunately, CRM centralizes the data trails required for such empirical optimization work.

By establishing continuous feedback loops linking lead management KPIs to insights that inform strategy adjustments, sales operations managers can systematically move the revenue needle over time. The key lies in analyzing bottlenecks, exploring causal relationships, testing changes and tracking impact. This data-driven optimization approach powered by CRM Reporting and Analytics is explored below.

Identifying Weak Links

A clear-eyed analytical review of the entire lead handling value chain is the necessary start. Which channels drive the most conversions? Where do opportunities stagnate and fall out of the pipeline most? Does sales follow best practice cadence for outreach? CRM reporting surfaces such breakdowns, revealing poor lead handoff coordination between teams, overwhelmed sales reps missing tasks, or ineffective nurture content as examples.

Diagnosing the Root Causes

Raw metrics simply show where outcomes underperform expectations, but don't explain why. Further scrutiny of associated lead attributes and engagement data surrounding the leaks can uncover the true drivers though. Does transition slippage concentrate among mid-market companies? Do closed deal cycles skew longer for public sector leads? These insights pinpoint addressable infrastructure gaps or process limitations to guide strategic priorities.

Instituting Targeted Changes

Optimization next involves designing and rolling out countermeasures tailored to root issue diagnoses. Steps might range from adjusting lead scoring models to better reflect qualifying behaviors unique to certain segments, building customized nurture tracks to sustain engagement among at-risk profiles, reallocating overburdened sales territories, or simply automating more handoffs to reduce human latency.

Tracking Impact Over Time

The final phase closes the loop. CRM reporting now validates whether instituted changes move the metrics in the right direction. Bouncing conversion rates, accelerated deal cycles, and reduced fallout indicate successes. But where targets remain unmet, the analysis cycle repeats, fine-tuning until all facets of lead management synchronize to support scalable sales growth.

Like an engine firing on all cylinders, tight integration across CRM-enabled lead management processes drives peak pipeline velocity and revenue performance. But no machine runs forever without a mechanic. Embedding iterative inspection, troubleshooting and enhancement through data-informed optimization creates a system continually tuned to reach its potential.

Chapter Nine

Sales Team Collaboration and Management

C ollaboration is essential for sales teams to maximize performance and meet revenue goals. However, fostering genuine collaboration can be challenging, especially in fast-paced sales environments. This article explores proven techniques leveraging CRM to promote sales team collaboration, streamline management, and ultimately drive better results.

A key advantage of CRM systems is breaking down silos by allowing company-wide transparency into sales interactions, accounts, and deals. Provide your entire sales team visibility into CRM records to facilitate information sharing and collaboration. Sales reps should be able to view details on accounts even if they are not the main point of contact to better support hand-offs and team selling.

The centralized database of customer interactions within CRM also presents opportunities for showcasing and sharing sales best practices across your team. Sales managers can highlight stellar call notes, creative pitch ideas, and other examples of excellence within CRM for all reps to review. When great ideas are visible for all, collaboration and healthy competition organically improves.

CRM also provides sales operations and management more effective oversight into sales rep activity and the ability to directly assign tasks to ensure execution of key sales plays. The system can track completion of assigned tasks set by sales leaders related to updates to account data, contact outreach, proposal creation, and other responsibilities tied to hitting quota. Higher visibility prevents drops and drives disciplined follow-up.

Driving Sales Team Collaboration with CRM

Effectively coordinating sales teams to execute strategies relies on laying out clear plans and guidelines within a robust CRM platform. This provides transparency into objectives plus oversight as tasks are completed by both individual reps and cross-functional units. Here's how you can leverage CRM for better team management:

Creating Detailed Sales Plans

Strategically planning out the sales process is essential for teams to systematically identify target accounts, craft appropriate outreach, execute effective campaigns, and secure customer wins. CRM systems provide robust functionality to create comprehensive sales plans directly tied to revenue goals. This transparency helps align cross-functional teams while systematizing execution.

Map Out Target Customer Profiles – CRM tools help sales leaders analyze historical deal data to identify ideal customer profiles with the highest propensity to purchase. Define target verticals, company sizes, budgets, and decision-maker roles and ensure this profile data is connected to accounts. This allows reps to segment and tier leads based on fit with proven winners.

Strategize Account-Based Outbound Campaigns – Granular account, contact, and lead data combined with integrated analytics in CRM also fuels more strategic outbound targeting. Sales ops and marketing can work together to upload targeted account lists, tag records, and develop customized sequences involving personalized messaging at scale. Reps receive notifications when their accounts engage to prompt timely follow-up.

Set Up Forecasting Models and Quotas – Robust CRM platforms make forecasting deal flow, modeling sales cycles, and assigning quota attainment goals more data-driven. Managements gets top-down visibility into projected versus actual sales activity segmented by rep, product line, and other dimensions while optimizing resource allocation.

Automate Next Step Recommendations – Sophisticated CRM systems leverage machine learning to prescribe next best actions for advancing opportunities based on historical account engagement patterns and activity metrics. These intuitive recommendations feed into planning outreach campaigns and defining lead nurturing sequences for consistent execution by reps.

Developing Step-by-Step Sales Playbooks

Highly effective sales teams rely on clearly documented playbooks of proven processes for critical initiatives like onboarding new customers. While static word documents and PDFs have limitations, CRM systems centralize these sales guidelines for ongoing optimization while embedded workflow functionality systemizes collaboration across departments.

Script Out Each Customer-Facing Interaction – Granular CRM platforms like Salesforce provide templates to script out step-by-step details required for executing sales strategies. Within account records, managers can outline all interactions their teams must have at each phase from initial calls, demonstrations, proposal presentations to negotiation and close.

Embed Collateral & Training Content – CRM ecosystems unite companywide resources for consistent delivery of messaging and content. Sales leaders can upload polished collateral including one-pagers, assessments, trial offers, contracts, and worksheets directly into relevant account records for immediate access by reps. Links to related training videos can drive self-enablement.

Auto-Assign Follow-Up Tasks in CRM – The system can also automatically create and assign next step tasks to keep new customer initiatives flowing based on defined playbooks. For example, after a Discovery Call, CRM can trigger an assigned task for the sales rep to update account details while notifying an SDR to schedule a product demo.

Notify Cross-Functional Teams Upon Milestones – In turn, CRM workflows can alert customer success, implementation specialists, IT, and other departments involved in onboarding of milestones reached. Once a deal reaches closed won status in CRM, automatic emails inform relevant colleagues to commence internal processes per their responsibilities in the playbook.

Streamlining Sales Teamwork with Tagging

As customer initiatives frequently involve cross-departmental collaboration, establishing clear roles and responsibilities in CRM systems provides vital structure. Strategic application of tags to accounts, contacts, leads and tasks denotes critical members of delivery teams while creating transparency around overall project health.

Tag Key Players by Department – Tag features classify records and tasks in CRM to quickly signal which internal stakeholders need visibility or action. As prospects move through sales stages, use tags to identify the migration team for implementation including Sales, IT, Customer Success, Finance personnel and more. Notification rules then auto-share updates based on tags.

Denote Cross-Functional Owners – For complex deals or accounts requiring intricate handoffs, tag feature allows labeling primary points of contact. Rather than vague "sales qualified lead" verbiage, tag "Account Manager" plus the individual's name directly in CRM record. This precision mitigates confusion of who owns next steps.

Track Project Status Tags – CRM systems can also assign tags like "Pending Approval", "Delayed", or "High Priority" to summarize overall project status without reading details. Leadership and operations can filter views on these progress indicators to course correct barriers more swiftly.

Prompt Interdepartmental Touchpoints – When used systematically across customer lifecycle, CRM tagging crystallizes hand-offs between sales, implementation, support and other groups. Workflow rules can mandate tags be applied at certain stages to prompt contact from downstream teams per service agreements.

Aligning Sales Teams with Shared Calendars

Keeping sales teams running in sync relies heavily on establishing unified visibility into the customer engagement calendar. CRM platforms like Salesforce integrate with popular calendar tools while allowing managers to oversee scheduling across reps. Shared appointment data fuels forecasting, surfaces conflicts and most importantly, orchestrates proactive outreach.

Automate Appointment Logging – A core obstacle sales leaders face remains reps failing to log meetings set. Integrations between CRM and email calendar systems like Outlook/G Suite automatically capture confirmed appointments. Regardless whether booked internally or via external email, the CRM calendar populates with scheduling details.

Spot Availability Gaps and Conflicts – Consolidating appointments from disparate tools provides managers clearer insight into rep bandwidth - or lack thereof. When the CRM calendar reflects heavy volumes of discovery calls, light training blocks present coaching opportunities. Leaders can also rapidly identify double-bookings across team members hampering collaboration.

Coordinate Customer Outreach – Shared customer engagement calendars fuel smarter opportunistic outreach between reps - especially for later stage opportunities requiring intricate orchestration. When a renewal negotiation with a strategic account appears on the calendar, teammates can schedule complementary value-building discussions.

Freeing Up Sales Teams with Process Automation

Sales leaders balancing complex initiatives look to leverage CRM systems to automate repetitive tasks. The technology now exists to systematize updates to records, assignment routing and customer communications allowing reps to focus on revenue-driving activities. When configured properly, automation enhances sales velocity, compliance and workforce collaboration.

Auto-Log Interactions in CRM – Despite constant customer calls and emails, manual logging of interactions falters as reps juggle competing priorities. CRM eliminates double data entry via integrations with email, dialers and calendar systems to automatically document talking points, objections and commitments.

Systematize Lead Assignment – Automated workflow rules can determine routing parameters for inbound leads based on territories, product specialties and workload balancing. Appropriate sales reps and SDRs receive assigned notifications without manager intervention to accelerate viable opps.

Trigger Personalized Customer Touches – CRM also streamlines recurring nurture and lifecycle campaigns via systems integration. Based on criteria like days since last contact or contract status change, the platform can activate sending tailored renewal offers, upsell promotions, or customer satisfaction surveys.

Unifying Sales Content and Access

The broader CRM platform has expanded beyond capturing customer interactions to provide centralized visibility across all vital information shaping deals. Tight integrations now connect email, spreadsheets, content repositories and more to CRM - with customized access by role - creating complete alignment.

Central Sales Content Hub – Native integrations between leading CRM solutions like Salesforce and cloud content platforms like Dropbox allow housing collateral, proposals, and onboarding paperwork natively alongside relevant account records for context. Bulk upload brand assets, strat guides and onboarding forms for instant access.

Permission Sales Guidelines – Granular permission settings in CRM also promote effective internal content governance. Specify that only regional sales VPs can modify global quoting calculators. Set new market entry assets visible to national sales team for feedback before external release.

Restrict Record Access – Just as permissions govern content access, CRM systems can customize visibility into accounts, contacts and deal data according to role. Executives may have a bird's eye dashboard spanning all revenue. Individual reps view primarily accounts and leads they directly own for compliance.

Optimizing Sales Team Performance

High-growth sales organizations inevitably reach an inflection point where tighter oversight and specialization unlocks the next level of results. Granular CRM systems provide the infrastructure to reassign contacts, customize metrics and reporting - ultimately accelerating revenue.

Reassign Contacts by Skillset – As the sales team expands, revisit contact assignments based on individual rep strengths, engagement history and capacity considerations. Does a longtime customer liaison better fit an enterprise rep? Would a junior team member have more touches for this small business account? CRM contact blocks enable strategic moves.

Redistribute Deals by Stage and Size – Similarly, scrub both open and closed/lost deals in CRM to shift opportunities to better aligned sales or customer success managers based on deal complexity and stage. Does this stalled opportunity indicate the need for executive leadership to renew dialogue? Does a big competitor win signal adjustments to target ideal customer profile?

Report on Metrics by User Group – To track the impact of reassignments and specialization, segment CRM data into teams, roles or personas for isolated analysis. Compare velocity through sales cycle by internal account manager vs channel partners. Assess renewal upsell conversion rates across retention specialists.

Driving Sales Excellence Through CRM

With sales leaders often struggling to balance strategy, personnel growth, and directly overseeing customer engagements, CRM delivers transparency to remotely coach and monitor team performance. Activity feeds chronicle rep interactions while pipeline reporting signals risks early for swift intervention.

Review Activity Streams for Insights – Robust CRM platforms like Salesforce include activity feeds displaying real-time chronological updates on critical events like calls, meetings, milestone changes, appointments scheduled and task completion. Rather than call/email each rep, managers review feeds to quickly gather customer momentum and engagement patterns.

Follow Team Pending Actions – Modern CRM also provides team activity overview where managers can filter on pending scheduled actions across their whole department or specific regions. This bird's eye calendar view reveals potential bottlenecks - like an overabundance of cancellations and reschedules - signaling deeper issues to address.

Set Revenue Forecasting Alerts – With arms around current sales activities, leaders must also implement rigorous CRM revenue forecasting alerts to receive notifications when projections shift in backlog stage changes. Sudden increases in "stalled deal" statuses should trigger inquiry into underlying obstacles for immediate intervention.

It is clear that CRM platforms have evolved to become essential sales acceleration engines - far surpassing the notion of mere databases for tracking interactions. Modern CRM solutions promote sales team collaboration through shared communication logs, calendars, and content. Integrations streamline manual tasks to give staff more capacity towards high-impact initiatives. Granular analytics combined with customizable permissions provide leadership increased visibility to optimize resource deployment against priority targets.

Ultimately, leveraging CRM as a centralized collaboration hub keeps teams aligned in even the most complex selling environments. Embedding playbooks and best practices into system workflows further reduces variability in execution. When responsibly embracing the latest AI-driven activity tracking, forecasting and recommendation tools, sales organizations operate more nimbly.

The future sales organization will continue advancing towards a landscape where technology fades to the background while alignment, productivity and effectiveness move to the fore. While CRM software provides the infrastructure, it remains the sales leaders effectively leveraging these tools to drive positive culture shifts who ultimately transform customer relationships and revenue performance.

Chapter Ten

Sales Reporting and Analysis

C ompleting the full sales cycle is as important as generating initial interest when engaging prospects. While enthusiasm and effort in sparking initial interest are invaluable, failing to carry opportunities through to closed sales is problematic. The inability to consistently close sales can frequently be attributed to missed opportunities already within your pipeline.

Implementing robust CRM sales reporting and analysis enables fact-based identification of risks and opportunities within your pipeline. Rather than relying solely on intuition, data-driven insights empower you to pursue optimization grounded in evidence.

Well-designed reports provide visibility into which prospects demonstrate purchase signals, where communication gaps exist that enable competitors to edge into your deals, and what trigger events consistently catalyze your buyers' decisions. Equipped with this level of clarity, you can reallocate time to propel promising opportunities forward and course-correct stagnating deals.

Beyond pipeline health, aggregated reporting offers crucial visibility into overall team performance. Tracking metrics like sales calls completed, first meetings scheduled, proposals delivered, and deals closed over specified time intervals paints a transparent picture of where productivity excels or lags. Understanding performance trends at both individual contributor and team levels enables targeted coaching and training to address skill gaps.

Additionally, properly contextualized data reveals where parts of your sales methodology may need reworking. If particular prospects consistently fail to close despite multiple proposals, your competitive positioning likely needs strengthening. If deals routinely get stuck at contract negotiation no matter the account, focusing legal support to simplify terms may be prudent.

Rather than leaving sales outcomes to "gut feel," robust analytics help organizational leaders make well-informed decisions. This methodical optimization of processes, messaging, and skill development is instrumental for driving sustainable revenue growth. Prioritizing CRM reporting and analysis can catapult your sales strategy to heights data ambiguity would never allow.

CRM Dashboards vs Reports

CRM systems contain a wealth of sales data spanning proposed deals, completed transactions, evolving customer relationships, and rep productivity. Converting these data points into actionable insights requires dedicated analysis using two primary tools: dashboards and reports.

Dashboards offer real-time, visual snapshots of key performance indicators relevant to sales workflows. Reports provide more extensive quantitative and qualitative scrutiny of sales outcomes, trends, and scenarios. Together, dashboards and reports constitute a powerful framework for optimizing decisions and strategy across sales teams and the wider organization.

Dashboards

Dashboards compress volumes of data into graphical interfaces that allow rapid recognition of patterns, outliers, and progress toward goals. Visual components like charts, graphs, gauges, and maps encoded with color draw the eye to changes and trends in key performance indicators.

Constructing a dashboard begins by isolating metrics integral for tracking sales outcomes. Common examples include:

- Sales pipeline progression by stage

- Revenue projections by month, quarter, or year

- Win rates for proposals delivered

- Average deal size and sales cycle duration

- Individual or team activities such as calls logged

Displaying these metrics visually elucidates their trajectories. For instance, a dashboard gauges representing each sales stage in the pipeline impart more immediacy to shrinking or expanding deals than percentages alone. Similarly, graphing quarterly revenue goals against actuals clearly demonstrates where performance gaps exist.

Benefits of dashboards include:

- Enabling snap decisions based on current standings

- Identifying outlying deals or reps for intervention

- Providing simplified progress communication to executives

- Motivating teams when goals remain within reach

With key data visualized, sales leaders can course-correct processes, realign team priorities, and allocate support resources to maintain momentum.

Reports

While dashboards focus primarily on surface-level awareness of sales vital signs, reports offer multidimensional analysis explaining why results manifest as they do. Reports compile traditional metrics with qualitative commentary, recommendations, and versatile presentation formats.

Common sales reports include:

- **Sales Funnel Analysis:** Studies conversion rates between pipeline stages. Identifies stages with significant fallout and suggests improvements to progress more prospects.

- **Sales Forecasts:** Compares revenue projections to actual income distributed across products, services, territories, customer segments etc. Calculates variance and assesses accuracy of existing forecasting models.

- **Win/Loss Analysis:** Breaks down why deals were won vs. lost. Tracks trends in competitive threats, pricing misalignments, feature gaps in offerings etc. that impact deal outcomes.

- **Sales Activities Analysis:** Logs number of daily calls, meetings, demonstrations, proposals etc. completed per rep. Highlights best practices from top performers.

Unlike static snapshots from dashboards, reports help leaders delve into granular details:

- Filter by date range, product, geography etc. to spotlight specific sales scenarios

- Export customizable PDF reports to distribute insights across the organization

- Split metrics by various parameters to pinpoint high and low performers

- Cross-tabulate data points to uncover causal relationships

These functionalities supply catalyzing evidence to execute strategies like expanding territories, reallocating quotas, or overhauling unsuitable messaging.

Maximizing Insights from Dashboards and Reports

While dashboards and reports serve complementary analytical purposes, their distinct capabilities drive unique benefits:

Dashboards

- Deliver quick overviews of sales health

- Enable timely interventions for outliers

- Simplify conveying progress to executives

- Motivate teams through visual goal pursuit

Reports

- Provide explanation through qualitative details

- Allow versatile filtering for tailored insights

- Export presentations to align wider organization

- Offer granular data to test hypotheses

An integrated approach leverages dashboards' brevity and visual potency for diagnosing issues. Reports then supply root cause investigation and prescriptive recommendations. Together, these tools provide comprehensive support for data-driven decision making across sales teams, surrounding departments, and organizational leadership.

Harnessing CRM Reporting to Unlock Sales Growth

For sales leaders seeking to optimize team strategy and performance, CRM reporting constitutes an invaluable asset. Granular analysis of rep activities, pipeline health, and revenue outcomes informs critical decisions guiding present operations and future growth.

The reporting tools detailed below represent indispensable managerial levers for monitoring and improving execution. Evaluating deal outcomes, buyer behaviors, personnel efficiency, and commission distribution through analytical CRM platforms establishes data-driven decision making. Robust reporting transforms opacity around sales processes into illuminating clarity that reveals optimization pathways. With these insights in hand, sales leaders can confidently guide strategies, teams, and systems toward sustaining success.

Evaluating Strategy with Core Sales Reports

CRM platforms integrate robust reporting to help managers weigh productivity, identify issues, and highlight winning strategies revealed through data. Four reports provide particular utility:

Win/Loss Analysis
Comparing trends across successful and failed deals produces a post-mortem that precipitates improvement. This report tallies proposals won versus those lost to competitors and surfaces patterns impacting outcomes. For example, consistent losses when bidding services against a rival may signal the need for competitive differentiation. Alternatively, losses confined to a particular region could indicate an underperforming sales rep requiring coaching.

Sales Forecasting
Using actualized outcomes, analytics engines within CRMs can project future revenue. Comparing forecasts to real-world figures allows frequent validation and refinement of predictive models. When large divergences emerge, inves-

tigating causal factors is prudent. External events like product shortages or internal realities like an understaffed sales team could be at play.

Pipeline Reporting

This functionality tracks deals spanning from initial discovery meetings to closed sales, delineating value and conversion rates across each of the defined sales stages. Monitoring phase-by-phase movement shows where prospects stagnate and fall out of the process. Managers can then formulate targeted interventions, whether improving technical demonstrations for the evaluation stage or adding legal support for contract finalizations.

Individual Rep Performance

Comparing productivity metrics for individual reps against team benchmarks helps managers tailor coaching and training. Metrics like call and email volumes, meetings booked, and proposals delivered showcase activity levels. Comparing this data to peers indicates where top performers excel and strugglers require guidance to achieve parity.

Customer-Focused Reports to Retain Accounts

Savvy sales leaders complement evaluations of internal workflows with intelligence centered on customer actions and sentiments. Two reports provide specially useful consumer perspectives.

Sales by Customer

By cataloging exact purchase histories across individual accounts and consumer segments, this functionality detects trends within buying behaviors. Users can filter date ranges and product types to identify seasonal sales surges, rising or falling purchases from key accounts, and top-consumed offerings. These insights feed targeted marketing campaigns and availability planning.

Customer Churn

Since acquiring new customers costs more than retaining existing ones, monitoring churn is prudent. This report calculates retention rates and the average lifetime value of current customers. Further analysis into churn root causes like price hikes, competitive encroachments, or diminished product quality enables course correction to improve satisfaction. Understanding churn dynamics also allows more accurate revenue forecasting.

Driving Performance with Activity Monitoring and Commission Tracking

Finally, CRM platforms contain reporting reflecting sales rep activity volumes and compensation performance. Both reports motivate teams, albeit through different means.

Sales Activity

This log of calls completed, meetings held, leads connected, and deals closed showcases worker engagement across individual reps and teams. Managers apply these productivity indicators to set performance targets, determine training needs, and highlight deserving top talent. Used positively, activity reporting fuels friendly performance competition and transparency around expected workloads.

Sales Commission

Outlining formulae and actual payouts calculated per sales representative ensures fair renumeration aligned to achievements. When reps understand exactly how rewards are earned, they can tailor daily workflows toward maximizing commissions under established organizational rules. Driving this incentivization fosters job satisfaction and higher incomes for stellar performers.

Every report has a particular frequency at which they are generated which can be monthly, quarterly or customized to the business's requirements.

Informing Strategic Decisions for Sales Leadership

Senior sales leaders occupy a unique vantage point, with responsibility for guiding organizational-wide strategy based on team performance within shifting market landscapes. Harnessing the robust analytic functionality of CRM systems enables precisely this oversight.

Among the multitude of available reports, several offer particular utility for executives balancing big-picture planning, enterprise risk management, and fostering sales growth.

The CRM reports detailed below move strategic decision-making for directors, VPs, and C-suite executives beyond hunches. Holistic productivity awareness, opportunity analysis, and consumer insights constitute an indispensable toolkit for leaders charting organizational growth trajectories. With these analytics firmly in hand, they can confidently guide teams, expansions, and optimizations rooted in empirical evidence.

Evaluating Omnichannel Sales Productivity

While frontline sales managers concentrate on supervising individual team metrics and initiatives, directors and VPs must interpret performance more broadly across the organization. Two comprehensive reports provide these cross-channel insights.

Sales Performance Dashboards

These visual snapshots consolidate multiple metrics into an instant overview of productivity, enabling rapid diagnosis of floundering areas. Typical dashboards combine data points like:

- Revenue/profit by product line and region

- Projected sales vs. actual

- Customer acquisition/loss rates

- Lead generation momentum

Interactively filtering by date ranges, demographics, or other variables elicits a flexibility unavailable in static reports. Performance dashboards empower VP-level leaders to pinpoint specific teams or geos to investigate further according to overarching growth strategies.

Sales Territory Analysis

Segmenting sales data by the regions, districts, or neighborhoods assigned to teams reveals macro-level patterns. When a particular city undergoes rapid revenue expansion or customer retention dramatically improves across a group of rural territories, investigating why provides replicable best practices. Furthermore, pairing territorial insights with broader demographic data helps leaders evolve expansion initiatives or marketing campaigns.

Strategic Pipeline and Revenue Planning

In addition to monitoring current progress, senior executives must perpetually plane future growth pursuits. Two reports provide vital intelligence to inform this long-view targeting.

Sales Funnel Analysis

While pipeline reporting surfaces deal progression at a superficial level, funnel analysis enriches superficial awareness with deal conversion benchmarks. Tracking stage-by-stage fallout helps executives identify where additional nurturing resources could catalyze opportunities into sales. Comparing conversion rates across territories or product lines also enables ongoing optimization based on strengths and weaknesses.

Revenue Forecasting and Modeling

Predicting sales volumes and profitability relies on advanced analytics engines within CRM platforms. These tools interweave historical performance, product line growth trends, seasonal variability, and other statistical inputs to project results by month, quarter, or year. As new data emerges, the models rapidly recalibrate projections accordingly. Monitoring forecast accuracy determines where enhancements may be beneficial.

Importantly, surfacing the key assumptions and risk factors incorporated into modeling promotes trust in forecast reliability across leadership stakeholders.

Promoting Sustainable Customer Relationships

While sustaining pipelines and revenue growth occupies the strategic spotlight, leaders must also construct durable customer relationships to ensure lasting success. Two reports especially aid these initiatives.

Customer Aging Analysis

This functionality categorizes customers across age segments based on first purchase date, average purchase frequency, last-known contact, and similar variables. Applying tailored outreach and support strategies across new, developing, and longtime customers promotes suitable relationship-building across the client lifecycle. Further parsing aging data by other traits like customer size or sector enables even more specialized nurturing.

Customer Churn Analysis

Calculating customer loss rates focuses retention efforts to curtail defections. Comparing churn metrics across customer segments, product categories, or support agents reveals where satisfaction lags and risks losing accounts. Similarly, contrasting churn between regions can spotlight potential issues with specific sales teams failing to establish rapport.

Overall, a forecast CRM report is a valuable tool for businesses to help sales leadership plan and manage their sales revenue. By using data from the company's CRM system and making informed assumptions, businesses can create realistic and actionable forecasts that can guide their decision-making and help them achieve their revenue targets.

Using CRM for Predictive Sales Analytics

For sales teams, securing deals hinges on proactively matching ideal solutions to emerging customer needs at precisely the right moments. An avalanche of data obscures vital signals required to consistently align these factors amidst dynamic markets. CRM analytics dissolve this barrier through predictive intelligence that clearly illuminates when, how, and to whom sales leaders should engage to drive conversions.

Here are some techniques for activating CRM data within predictive engines, outlining methodology, intelligence types, and key business applications. With these insights, sales organizations can evolve reactive processes into predictive workflows fine-tuned for seizing opportunities.

Methodology: Data Inputs to Prediction Outputs

Ingesting dispersed CRM data, predictive tools analyze historical deal patterns in search of correlations that reveal future likelihood. Common data feeds include:

- Product selections by customer segment

- Unclosed deal details and bottlenecks

- Purchase frequency patterns and seasonality

- Comparison engagement rates across channels

Statistical modeling applied to these inputs identifies sequences likely to recur given similar conditions. For example, the tool may determine companies of a certain size and sector often pursue 20% discounting after a set number of email nurtures over several months.

These probabilistic insights then guide sales actions aligned to the predicted optimal approach. As new deal data emerges, predictions undergo constant refinement toward ever-increasing accuracy.

Intelligence for Informed Human Decisions

Rather than replacing human judgement outright, predictive intelligence serves to better inform selling strategy not easily intuable otherwise. Three output types empower more calculated actions:

Deal Risk Scoring

Assessing proposal likelihood of success or failure given nuances like product fit, buyer budget, and competitive elements assists planning. Reps can pursue promising opportunities more aggressively while mitigating resource waste chasing unlikely deals.

Purchase Timing Estimates

By indicating periods when customers may be more inclined to buy, reps can better time engaging communications to seasons of increased receptiveness. The tool effectively acts as an automated trigger alerting reps to prime moments.

Channel/Message Matching

Guidance detailing optimal channels and framing for outreach helps reps break through the noise in crowded inboxes. Pitching by the customer's preferred channel and emphasizing aligned messaging boosts conversion potential.

Driving Revenue Growth with CRM Predictive Analytics

Forwarding-looking sales leaders increasingly embrace predictive intelligence to sharpen competitive positioning. By revealing subtle opportunity signals within

CRM data, predictive tools guide more calculated selling strategies personalized to each customer's inclinations.

Finding Opportunity in Data

Effective predictive analytics applies statistical modeling and machine learning algorithms to historical CRM data in search of patterns predictive of future deal outcomes. Typical data ingested includes:

- Product preferences across customer demographics

- Deal negotiation processes and bottlenecks

- Buying cycles and seasonal purchase variability

- Engagement/response rates by communication channel

Crunching this training data, analytics tools discern subtle correlations between behaviors, attributes, and deal results. These insights fuel opportunity recommendations fine-tuned to each prospect based on similarities to past won opportunities. As tools ingest new data from successful deals, recommendations grow ever more accurate.

Solving Key Sales Challenges Through CRM Analytics

Embedding actionable intelligence across CRM systems alleviates a multitude of sales obstacles, including:

Increasing Win Rates

Deal risk scoring highlights proposal weaknesses early while directing resources only toward worthwhile opportunities expected to convert. Increased insight improves resource allocation efficacy.

Optimizing Sales Capacity

Determining ideal customer contact timing and appropriate messaging frameworks maximizes the impact of touchpoints. Reduced misfiring leaves more capacity for strategic engagement.

Prioritizing Accounts

Identifying lookalike audiences primed for products based on previous buyer journeys assists targeting. Precise prospect selection alleviates wasted effort.

Forecasting Revenue

Understanding periodic purchase cycles improves annual projections by revealing expected peaks and valleys. Models also quantify pipeline health and bottlenecks.

Expanding Business Intelligence

Unlike static reporting reflecting just singular sales snapshots, predictive analytics undergo constant improvement from ongoing user input. As sales reps log CRM updates like deals won, lost, or stalled, they provide feedback to refine underlying statistical models powering opportunity recommendations.

This allows tools to rapidly learn and improve suggestions over time through correlations between behaviors, interventions, and outcomes. Continual expert feedback thus expands analytical sophistication beyond what any manual analysis could feasibly achieve.

Predictive analytics inject CRM platforms with the contextual intelligence required to determine smart account targeting strategies and identify ripe revenue possibilities. Translating opaque data signals into transparent opportunity roadmaps guides today's sales leaders to smarter decisions and faster growth.

Chapter Eleven

Overcoming Challenges in Adoption

I mplementing a CRM system can provide immense value by centralizing your customer data, enabling stronger analytics, and streamlining sales processes. However, without thoughtful adoption, a CRM can fail to deliver on its promise and potentially reduce productivity.

As the sales operations leader responsible for maximizing CRM impact, you need to be aware of common implementation challenges. Selecting an inflexible platform unfit for your workflows or failing to properly integrate and customize it can undermine user adoption. Repetitive manual data entry and disconnected systems lead to wasted time without revenue gains.

While these pitfalls may seem discouraging, they can be preempted through an informed, user-focused approach. This chapter will equip you to spearhead a successful deployment by:

- Illustrating must-know adoption challenges

- Providing techniques to avoid or overcome them

- Sharing actionable best practices for configuration and change management

By preparing for the realities of CRM onboarding, educating your teams, and emphasizing organizational alignment, you will be primed to unlock the many rewards of an integrated sales technology ecosystem. Now let's explore key obstacles and how to turn them into opportunities.

Driving CRM Adoption Across Your Sales Organization

While over 90% of companies utilize CRM platforms, many fail to realize their full potential due to limited user adoption. Without staff buy-in and comprehensive usage, CRMs cannot provide the complete visibility and workflow streamlining they promise.

As the sales operations leader, the CRM's impact hinges on your ability to motivate adoption. This requires surmounting common hurdles like change resistance and misunderstood value. By proactively addressing barriers with training and support, you can transform sales behaviors to fully leverage your CRM investment.

Understanding The Adoption Challenge

Despite the proliferation of CRM solutions, sales professionals continue facing adoption obstacles:

- 52% of sales leaders state their CRM results in lost opportunities. Why? Data gaps from poor usage undermine analytics and forecasting.

- 50% of companies cannot access a unified customer view across functions, preventing informed outreach. Silos emerge absent enterprise-wide contribution.

- 48% report misalignment between their CRM and sales processes. Without customization, systems disrupt rather than enhance workflows.

Given this reality, your personnel likely harbor doubts about yet another software rollout. They may view the CRM as an administrative chore offering little personal utility.

These sentiments breed avoidance and workarounds that can seriously inhibit success. But you have the power to shift mindsets through strategic change leadership.

Best Practices For Driving Adoption

To guide your sales organization to embrace CRM best practices, leverage the following proven techniques:

Illustrate Direct Value

Begin by connecting the dots between CRM utilization and improved sales outcomes. For example, highlight how activity logging and pipeline visibility enables more precise forecasting to systematically grow deals. With a CRM's holistic context, reps can also coordinate handoffs, share intelligence, and expand account potential. Tangibly demonstrate how these capabilities translate into career benefits through recognition, promotions, and higher commissions.

Deliver Ongoing Training

Comprehensive training sets the stage for proficient usage. Break training into digestible components that can be sustained long-term, like quick self-service content modules and microlearning apps. Offer one-on-one coaching and office hours to address individual gaps. Send regular tip emails, host refresh webinars, and make sure new hires are immediately up to speed.

Incentivize Through Gamification

Introduce leaderboards, points systems, badges, and rewards programs to motivate engagement. Publish individual and team adoption metrics along with successes to foster healthy competition. Highlight top performers and celebrate usage milestones publicly. Consider tying software proficiency and data quality directly to compensation and advancement decisions.

Monitor Adoption Continuously

Leverage your CRM's activity logging to trace utilization rates. Conduct intermittent audits of data health, looking for gaps indicating underuse. Seek direct user feedback through surveys and interviews to pinpoint adoption barriers. Then create targeted assistance, whethersupplementary education or simplified functionality for common pain points. Appoint "CRM Champions" across sales teams to surface concerns and model best practices.

Driving adoption requires understanding stakeholder mindsets and matching support strategies accordingly. But with the right leadership, your CRM will transform into a valued asset for sustaining sales growth.

Bridging Interdepartmental Divides

A CRM system's centralized database only delivers value when powered by comprehensive, accurate data. With scattered adoption across functions, critical information gaps emerge – degradingVisibility and enabling misalignment. This leaves sales teams disconnected, buried in redundant administrative tasks rather than executing high-impact initiatives.

As the orchestrator of sales operations, the onus falls on you to foster enterprise-wide participation. This begins by addressing the root causes of poor cross-functional cooperation to reshape behaviors. By spotlighting inefficient workflows and barriers to communication, you can implement targeted change management programs for maximizing coordination.

Defining The Communication Challenge

Flawed CRM data quality typically links back to internal divisions between departments. Sales often operates in an isolated bubble, missing critical customer insights from marketing or service interactions. 11% of sellers lack basic CRM understanding, leading to misuse and gaps. Further breakdowns include:

- Conflicting customer data spreading as sales and marketing tools remain disconnected, creating misleading profiles.

- Poor visibility into account activity outside sales interactions hinders context and follow-up coordination.

- Information held locally on spreadsheets, independant systems or even paper means manual efforts to consolidate a unified view of accounts and progress.

- No established protocols for keeping centralized CRM records updated in terms of personnel changes, contact details, conversation histories, scheduled tasks and action items.

This breeds a culture of misaligned priorities and inefficient handoffs between sales, marketing and customer service. Valuable time redirects towards reconciling discrepancies and information requests rather than revenue-focused work.

Strategies For Improving Cross-Departmental Collaboration

The key to dismantling departmental divides lies in targeted initiatives that incentivize unified CRM usage. By spotlighting shared objectives, structuring consistent data requirements, opening communication channels, and promoting collaborative behaviors, silos dissolve into an integrated ecosystem. Let's explore techniques for executing each approach:

Spotlight Shared Objectives

The foremost barrier stems from functional teams lacking appreciation for how cohesive CRM adoption furthers collective goals. Sales may resist logging interactions if they fail to see downstream impact on win rates. Service reps won't prioritize entering case summaries if not aware it informs account planning. By showcasing cross-departmental use cases, you can realign mindsets:

- Demonstrate how sales activity feeds targeted marketing campaigns that expand awareness at key accounts.

- Show customer service teams how access to historic sales discussions prevents repetition and enables personalized issue resolution.

- Explain to executives how end-to-end visibility drives more calculated growth investments and retention programs.

Use tangible examples of how fragmented efforts undermine shared gains, contrasted with unified successes. This empowers personnel as stakeholders in the CRM's overall success.

Structure Data Requirements

Conflicting data standards across functions quickly snowball into intelligence gaps that exacerbate misalignment. But by governing standardized vocabulary, mandatory fields, activity classifications and account lifecycles, accuracy improves. Codify data protocols through system settings, procedural checklists, data integrity validations, and quality tracking. Then monitor adoption while offering supplemental training to solidify consistency.

Open Communication Channels

Although departments may conceptualize CRM capabilities differently, building bridges prevents disconnects. Establish monthly or quarterly cross-functional working sessions for advice sharing around feature usage strategies. Implement omni-channel referral flows so service can automatically route sales-ready leads. Integrate collaborative tools like file sharing and internal chat features to dismantle isolation.

Incentivize Alignment

Once the above channels take hold, further motivate participation through incentivized goal setting. Establish distinct targets for cross-team referrals, knowledge base contribution, and data accuracy. Recognize top collaborators through internal marketing and rewards programs. Even consider tying compensation directly to interdepartmental CRM utilization to tangibly move the needle.

With these multidimensional strategies, CRM adoption transforms into a vehicle for organizational cohesion and clarity. This emerges from a culture centered on openness, transparency, and unified progress tracking.

Selecting an Optimized CRM Solution Aligned to Your Needs

Implementing a CRM system marks a major investment aimed at enhancing sales efficiency. But with countless options boasting unique capabilities at varying price points, inadequate research often results in a mismatch between software strengths and organizational requirements. This abandons ROI and progresses little beyond the status quo.

By taking a methodical approach tuned to your workflows, teams, and objectives, you can identify the ideal platform. This requires an introspective analysis of existing inefficiencies, an examination of stakeholder needs, and an avoidance of feature overload. With the right CRM, data consolidates, tasks automate, and personnel unify around providing seamless customer experiences.

Defining Your Technology Gap

The CRM selection process begins by spotlighting current process limitations and intelligence gaps impeding growth. As Chapter 1 outlines, cross-functional working sessions focused on these pain points illuminate true requirements. Common limitations include:

- Visibility Struggles: Siloed datasets across systems yield an incomplete view of customer health and account history. This breeds misaligned outreach.

- Reporting Issues: With transactional data spread broadly, sales leadership lacks holistic reporting to pinpoint refinement opportunities.

- Administrative Inefficiencies: Manual processes like contact data entry, activity logging, and task management divert focus from revenue-driving activities.

Be thorough in documenting where workflows breakdown, data frays, and teams miscommunicate. This forms the foundation for building a targeted request for proposals.

Conducting an Unbiased CRM Assessment

Once the business has defined the ideal future state, systematically evaluate marketplace options of CRM systems available against critical selection criteria without bias towards flashy features. Central parameters include:

- Pricing: Compare setup, licensing models, and required infrastructure against budgets.

- Existing Workflows: Ensure flexible customization and intuitive UX for user adoption.

- Data Structure: Guarantee integration potential across essential databases for a 360-degree customer view.

- Future Roadmap: Seek a long-term oriented partner for scaling needs.

Chapter 2 provides a detailed methodology for this process. But the key lies in prioritizing must-haves over nice-to-haves. A pricing sheet loaded with irrelevant tools suggests a poor fit.

Tuning Solutions to Stakeholders

Every department leverages CRM capabilities differently. Marketing may value automation around lead scoring workflows based on campaign interactions. Service needs case management and resolution tracking functionalities. Sales focuses on contact management and opportunity pipeline visibility.

But a siloed view breeds impractical trade-offs, so you need a comprehensive understanding across roles. Engage each group to map software priorities before aligning on a unified recommendation.

This prevents an overload of unused features while optimizing for cross-departmental adoption. Reconcile desires by identifying the highest mutual return on investment based on pain point severity.

Implementing with the End Goal in Mind

A CRM that appears well-equipped today may overlook evolving needs down the road. So adopt a visionary mindset when evaluating future scalability. Ensure open APIs and integration standards are in place for interoperating with adjacent solutions as workflows mature.

ebenfalls, understand that realize ROI means configuring beyond out-of-box settings. Allocate resources appropriately for customized migrations, data integrity testing, and user training essential for sticking the landing.

By taking an introspective approach to align technology with processes, people, and business objectives, you amplify opportunity for CRM success. Following structured selection best practices prevents the pitfalls of purchasing generalization in favor of strategic specialization.

Breaking Down Data Silos Through CRM and System Integration

A CRM system represents a central hub connecting sales processes to underlying customer intelligence. But when platforms operate in isolation, restricted data sharing leads multiple versions of the truth emerge across teams. Sales leadership then loses visibility into performance while service and marketing remain disconnected from account history needed to personalize engagement.

Fortunately, modern infrastructure and middleware make CRM and external system integration more seamless than ever. By unifying data lakes into collaborative oceans, you prevent redundancy and misalignment. This requires understanding common integration methods for syncing platforms, mitigating risks of blending datasets, and matching techniques to complexity.

Defining the Silos

Before executing integration, map current data fractures across essential systems. Core disconnects include:

Transactional Data Silos – Order, invoice and payment data often siloes in accounting platforms like NetSuite rather than funneling into customer records within the CRM for usability across functions. This limits commercial insight.

Marketing Technology Silos – Platforms like Marketo and Hubspot feature their own contact databases, campaign analytics and lead scoring capabilities which sales teams lack access to for enhancing outreach.

Service Silos -Help desk systems containing support ticket history operate detached from account visibility. Preventing reference during renewal conversations or upsell discussions.

Start by documenting where these gaps exist between key sales, marketing and operational systems relative to your CRM. Understanding pain points helps shape infrastructure strategy.

Bridging Data Silos Through Targeted Integration

Once dysfunction created by disjointed systems is spotlighted, bridge gaps using methods tuned to infrastructure complexity. Balance accessibility against governance to enable unified intelligence. Critical techniques include:

Lightweight Links

For supplementary platforms like analytics with limited datasets, basic API links allow useful activity syncing without risky overexposure. This prevents sales teams from manual exports while still restricting access to temporary campaign databases. Govern usage by restricting API keys to specific modules and read-only permissions. Monitor link failures causing stalled data flows. Schedule recurring reviews on link viability as needs evolve.

Embedded Integrations

When sales enablement and learning systems contain proprietary methodology or regulated content, embed targeted integrations. Bi-directional data flows between specific CRM and platform modules then enable customized recommendations while limiting visibility.

Sales governance committees grant access through segmented provisioning rules and profiles. Monitor utilization rates and manual data re-entry indicating poor adoption. As new modules launch, reassess integration schematics against updated architecture.

Middleware Pipelines

In complex legacy ecosystems involving on-premise ERPs, middleware acts as a intermediary conduit for handling bulk batch data migration. IT implements standardized schema linking models while data teams handle transformation rules enabling sales data warehousing. This allows large transactional system connectivity without risky overexposure.

Govern usage through fixed integration runtime schedules, exception handling for stalled batches, and qiuality checks post-migration. Create formal change management procedures for addressing evolving analytics needs requiring modifications to the configured extract-transform-load (ETL) process.

Access Model Segmentation

Balance usability with security by tiering access. Read-only general visibility prevents sales data tampering while interim sandbox testing environments allow exploratory analysis without production impact on live systems. Strictly control sandbox entry through access request ticketing procedures mandated by data stewards.

Compliance Standards

Enterprises with regulated data in fields like healthcare and finance require integrating platforms certified to stringent controls. Formally assess security, encryption and access protocols generally through questionnaires. Create an audit trail documenting provider self-attested compliance against configured linkages.

With progressive governance applied based on integration complexity, overlapping yet secure connections bridge gaps efficiently. The key is crafting maintainable yet adaptable links between platforms and departments crucial to the customer journey.

Ensuring CRM Data Integrity Through Governance and Validation

A CRM system represents a single source of truth on customer interactions, health, and revenue trajectories. But with under 80% average data accuracy according to Validity's research, misinformation drives misaligned outreach. Preventable losses then persist from stalled deals to customer erosion.

Restoring confidence requires acknowledging the customer data lifecycle. As personnel transition and account details evolve, new inputs risk tainting existing records. So you need governance policies ensuring changes undergo appropriate verification through:

Access Controls

Misupdates often link to uncontrolled CRM access allowing unvalidated changes. Define system roles granting tiered writing privileges to enforce separation of duties. For example, sales representatives may append activity logs while data administrators exclusively modify foundational details like changed account ownership.

Workflow Constraints

Further systematize changes by configuring field-level logic dictating allowable inputs. When phone updates batch upload, mandate they pass verification checks against carrier records before committing updates. Introduce tiered approval chains for changes beyond defined thresholds to prompt manual review.

Validation Cycles

Schedule periodic data reviews to quantify completeness, accuracy, and consistency across fields prone to fragmentation over ongoing usage. Establish data quality KPIs like discrepancy rates per object tying back to data stewards for issue resolution. Leverage both system validations and manual auditing.

Master Data Foundation

Centralize storage of verified "golden record" data like normalized account and contact details. Propagate from this master dataset into downstream systems through batch push or access APIs to supersede chances of redundancy across tools. This accelerates system consolidation efforts.

Ongoing Training

Reinforce protocols through initial and refresher training highlighting the downstream implications of misinformation. Incentivize vigilance by incorporating data health metrics into staff evaluation criteria.

With the right symbiosis of process and technology governing system input, output and storage, data integrity restores confidence in underlying CRM intelligence. This shifts focus fully towards capitalizing on analytical potential.

Securing Executive Buy-In

While CRM solutions promise immense utility by tracking customer interactions, leadership approval depends on positioning technology investments as profit drivers rather than cost centers. So the onus falls on sales operations to craft a compelling vision translating efficiency into revenue. This requires quantitative ROI projections and adoption management plans that assuage concerns around wasted spending or inadequate usage.

With meticulous financial analysis and operational transparency, you can rally executives around CRM transformation to unlock profitability previously hindered by human limitations. Now let's review framing strategies for earning leadership endorsement critical for implementation success.

Spotlighting Current Inefficiencies

Document exactly how disjointed systems, opaque visibility, and misaligned staff priorities currently restrain income growth. Contextualize with data comparing performance against industry benchmarks. Common pitfalls include:

Poor Handoff Accountability - Outdated spreadsheets and email-based handoff protocols between sales stages result in 44% of leads slipping through the cracks in absence of centralized tracking.

Inaccessible Knowledge - With account history and planned renewals scattered across individual hard drives, 13% of deals stall from missing contextual references during negotiations.

Stalled Productivity - Manual administrative tasks like data entry and activity logging consume 32% of the average sales representative's time instead of high-impact account outreach.

Attach hard figures around lost deals, shortened sales cycles, and reduced administrative hours to showcase current constraints. This informs leadership on addressable gaps.

Modeling the CRM ROI Payoff

Armed with baseline inefficiency data, contrast today's state against the CRM's future benefits. As Nucleus found, $1 in CRM spending returns $8.71 through enhanced sales productivity and retention. But you must translate assumptions into an auditable financial model rooted in organizational change. Components include:

- Baseline Sales Forecast: Project next year's revenue based on current metrics

- Risk-Adjusted Upside: Overlay expected CRM impact on win rates, productivity hours recovered, and expanded account capacity

- Implementation Cost Schedules: Breakdown one-time and ongoing licensing, infrastructure, customization and support expenses

- Adoption Rate Models: Gradually phase-in benefits over 12 months based on change management planning

The output is a datadriven ROI forecast verifying profitable investment backing leadership approval.

Communicating the Operational Transformation Journey

While financially prudent on paper, CRM success depends on widespread user adoption across sales teams enhancing data quality. So accompany ROI forecasts with an operational roadmap addressing leadership anxieties around execution. Elements include:

- Deployment Timeline: Plot phased rollout grouping similar roles to maximize initial training efficiency

- Milestone Tracking: Establish usage, data health and pipeline conversion metrics demonstrating incremental returns

- Support Resources: Allocate help desk, online tutorials, and coaching budgets to drive proficiency

- Training Curriculum: Outline required participation criteria and competency certification enforcing adoption

- Risk Management: Define fallback plans like limited license renewals for missed targets due to unforeseen change resistance

This illustrates your grasp over navigating organizational shifts from software installation through ROI realization. Your thoroughness builds stakeholder confidence.

With credible financials and operations management planning demonstrating mastery, leadership eagerly transitions from the status quo towards CRM empowerment. Quantify the future while showing you have the capacity to methodically transform sales vision into reality.

Chapter Twelve

Best Practices

Today's platforms are more sophisticated than ever, armed with advanced analytics, automation and integrations that simply didn't exist even a few years ago. However, while the technology has rapidly evolved, many sales organizations still struggle to realize the full potential from their CRM investments. There are a few key reasons why sales teams fail to maximize value from their customer relationship platforms:

- Misalignment on goals and metrics tied to customer relationship initiatives

- Inadequate change management and user adoption strategies

- Attempting advanced functionality before mastering the basics

- Not keeping pace with new features and capabilities

- Poor data quality diluting insights and recommendations

This chapter provides a practical roadmap for sales operations leaders looking to elevate customer relationships and sales performance through a customer relationship platform. We will cover everything from getting executive alignment, to driving adoption in the field, to advancing from basic reporting into predictive analytics.

While today's tools offer tremendous capabilities, realizing value requires much more than just software. With the right vision, leadership and discipline, you can harness the power of your customer relationship investment to strengthen customer loyalty, empower your sales teams and gain a competitive edge. These are the key steps and best practices to make that vision a reality.

Set Defined CRM Objectives

A critical yet often overlooked aspect of developing an impactful CRM strategy is defining clear, measurable goals aligned to overarching business objectives. Well-defined CRM goals provide direction, allow you to benchmark progress, motivate teams, and ultimately elevate sales performance and customer experience. This chapter will explore best practices for setting robust CRM goals, gathering stakeholder input, and connecting goals to value creation.

Align CRM Goals to Business Objectives

The success of a CRM hinges on how well it helps you achieve strategic business outcomes. Start by identifying 3-5 priority business objectives the CRM must support, whether it's boosting revenue by 15%, increasing customer retention by 20% or improving sales cycle efficiency by 30%. Contextualizing CRM goals is key to ensuring implementation stays focused on tangible value vs. just technology management.

Boosting Sales Performance

For almost all organizations, the foremost CRM objective is driving higher sales results. Be specific by defining numeric targets for metrics like lead conversion rates, deal sizes, sales cycle velocity, and overall revenue growth. Cascade sales goals throughout the pipeline, clarifying expectations for lead generation, nurturing, qualification and closed deals.

Enhancing Customer Experience

While critical, sales numbers alone don't reflect client relationships. Set objectives for improving key customer experience metrics like Net Promoter Scores (NPS), satisfaction levels, retention/loyalty and share of wallet. Connect CX goals to revenue impact by modeling potential gains with increased retention or larger average deal sizes.

Increasing Efficiency

An effective CRM significantly improves sales efficiencies by enhancing productivity, collaboration and automation. Define efficiency KPIs like calls per rep per day, win rates, proposals delivered on time, reporting throughput and content reuse. Attach specific and measurable goals like 20% more calls daily or cutting reporting time by 4 hours per week.

Gaining Data Insights

Rich, accurate customer data is arguably a CRM's greatest asset. Set objectives to realize that potential via robust analytics capabilities plus easily-accessible, role-based reporting. Establish adoption targets for dashboards and self-service portals. Set goals based on key insights needed to guide strategy.

Rallying the Organization

The best CRM objectives incentivise action while being realistically achievable. Make sure corporate leadership endorses top-tier goals and that account teams have input into quota and pipeline targets. Maintain visibility through published goal matrices and reports tracking progress towards success metrics. Recognize wins and address obstacles promptly.

Connecting Goals to Value

Ultimately CRM goals exist to drive business value. Maintain focus on the end-game by continuously reaffirming key value drivers. Model target metrics' financial implications through techniques like calculating the revenue impact of a 10% lift in retention. Illustrate how smarter cross-selling through improved account insights may increase share of wallet by 30%. Correlating CRM goals to monetary value provides compelling motivation and justification for meeting (and funding) objectives.

Well-conceived CRM goals provide necessary direction to implementation initiatives while enabling transparency into value realization. Mark success by the degree goals reflect strategic priorities, incent action, and translate into enhanced sales and customer excellence. Defining the right CRM objectives requires insight, inclusion and perspective, but pays dividends through optimized technology use plus improved organizational alignment and performance.

Execute an Organized CRM Launch

The most strategically-sound CRM investment can flounder due to poor execution. Conversely, even basic solutions can deliver value if backed by an effective implementation plan addressing critical areas like staffing, requirements, data and user adoption. This section outlines best practices for launching your CRM to achieve maximum benefit.

Assembling the Launch Team

Start by establishing a strong governance structure with engaged stakeholders and clear decision rights. Appoint an executive sponsor to champion the initiative, align priorities and resolve issues. Designate an experienced project manager to handle planning and daily execution. Populate the launch team with subject matter experts in sales, marketing, service and analytics to specify needs. Including program managers and end-users provides essential perspective.

Defining Solution Requirements

Conduct workshops with launch team members to detail critical requirements across features, technology and commercial considerations. Document must-have capabilities like lead scoring, opportunity management and configurable reporting essential for value realization. Specify any needed third-party integrations for data syncing, identity management etc. Outline budgetary guardrails and criteria for provider selection. Trace all specifications back to core CRM goals so resulting solutions directly support desired outcomes.

CRM Software Evaluation

With requirements established, research vendors to identify optimal platforms. Allow launch team members to participate in demos and trials to assess functional fit along with factors like usability and support options. Soliciting user feedback fosters buy-in. Validate claimed capabilities through scripted testing. Complete due diligence on vendors through reference checks and financial reviews to minimize risk. Structure contracts favorably using insights from requirements gathering to maximize flexibility and incentives like performance-based pricing.

Data Integration & Migration

Many CRM initiatives falter due to data-related issues. Invest heavily upfront in proper data governance, infrastructure and mapping specifications. Assess existing data stores' accessibility, integrity and alignment to new system parameters. Enact required integrations, allowing adequate testing periods. Account for transition considerations relative to legacy tools and migration timelines. Data should never be an afterthought when implementing a modern CRM—arm your launch team to own readiness here.

Training, Testing & Change Management

The best platforms still fail absent thoughtful adoption strategies addressing people, process and skills-building. Make training mandatory at launch using customized content reflecting actual workflows. Devote 20% of go-live timeframes exclusively for testing real scenarios and user feedback incorporation. Reinforce change management through consistent executive messaging and embedded user assistance. View the launch as an evolution rather than a hard cutoff—be patient but focused in propelling utilization forward.

Govern Performance Post-Launch

Transitioning from implementation to ongoing optimization is equally important for CRM success. Establish mechanisms to continuously collect user feedback. Create adoption dashboards tracking usage across system components. Build regular reviews of goal progress into staff meetings at multiple levels. Use insights to expand features being leveraged, address barriers to adoption and right-size investments on an ongoing basis—keeping the CRM tuned to current needs.

Effective CRM delivery requires meticulous implementation planning spanning solution configuration, data readiness, skill-building and governance. Right-size investments here to match platform complexity and change management needs. Ultimately, measured launches enable organizations to maximize value from their customer management capabilities. For more information on implementation, refer to Chatper 3.

Optimize CRM Relevance Through Customization

Off-the-shelf CRM platforms build in flexibility to accommodate varying needs, but rarely deliver perfect out-of-box alignment. Thankfully, leading solutions offer customization tools empowering organizations to cost-effectively adapt systems to their environments. These are some techniques for enhancing CRM relevance through focused customization while balancing complexity and total cost of ownership.

Prioritizing Custom Capabilities

Resist over-customization by targeting high-impact areas where base functions miss the mark while leaning on vendor strengths elsewhere. Audit your process and data landscapes, noting inputs, outputs and pain points for each persona and workflow. Review desired reports, metrics and integrations supporting objectives. Cross-reference gaps against solution functionality to identify cus-

tomization candidate areas related to data structure, user experience and analytics. Size opportunities according to impact and difficulty to inform roadmap
prioritization.

Common Customization Areas

While needs vary across businesses, most find value tailoring certain elements
around data capture, workflow enhancement and reporting. Supplementary
data fields allow capturing previously unavailable yet operationally-critical information like regional regulatory requirements or channel-specific costs. Additional process triggers and alerts improve routing and oversight, ensuring
the right interactions reach the right people. Custom dashboards, reporting
packages and integration feeds unlock deeper insights for decision-making.

Leveraging Configuration over Coding

Look to leverage user-accessible configuration tools before pursuing hard-cod-
ing changes which increase complexity. Solutions like Zoho and Salesforce
enable administrators to selectively adjust field names, options, validations,
page layouts, object relationships, automation rules, record types, data access
permissions and more through simple wizards and drag-and-drop UIs. Take
advantage of APIs and built-in integration platforms requiring only lightweight
configuration for connections. Save custom software development for scenarios
lacking alternative build options. Minimizing bespoke modifications reduces
maintenance overhead and system brittleness over time while still expanding
relevance.

Supplementary Apps & Components

Robust CRM app marketplaces provide access to hundreds of plug-and-play
tools addressing nearly any gaps unfilled during initial software evaluations.
Evaluate connectors for ecosystems like Slack, Microsoft and Google along with
utilities improving reporting, analytics and field-specific workflows. Lean on
apps to quickly obtain wanted capabilities vs. costly development efforts. Be

judicious installing components receiving mixed reviews or lacking clear vendor support models. Only pay for what you require while prioritizing stability.

Measuring Customization ROI

Approach investments in custom-enhancing your CRM solution as you would any other project—requiring clear ROI justification, measurable results and governance. Establish processes for collecting user feedback and quantifying efficiency gains, revenue increases or cost reductions attributable to added capabilities. Publicize quick wins like improved sales data accuracy while socializing a roadmap for addressing functionality gaps long-term. Ensure customizations map back to core CRM goals at every stage rather than "nice to have" feature bloat.

Right-sized customization delivers outsized impact by optimizing CRM relevance to your specific needs and workflows. Focus enhancements on high-value coverage gaps using simplified configuration tools before custom coding. Continuously confirm additions drive towards strategic goals to maximize ROI in elevating sales, service and operational performance through a tailored CRM platform. Alignment and adoption thrive when systems feel purpose-built rather than one-size-fits-all. To further learn about customizing your CRM, refer to Chapter 4.

Ensure Data Integrity

A CRM's potential directly correlates to the quality of its underlying data. Messy, inaccurate information severely impedes reporting and analytics, eroding trust and adoption. By contrast, robust data governance policies promoting integrity across key elements like validity, accuracy, consistency and completeness establish confidence while enabling impactful insights.

Establishing Data Standards

Start by enacting data policies aligned to strategic goals. Define standards for critical fields like customer contact details, product classifications, channel definitions, regional groupings etc. Leverage validation rules and mandatory formats to reinforce compliance, preventing bad data at the source vs. fixing issues post-entry. Appoint data stewards to formally govern taxonomies and resolve gray areas for complex categories like sales stage probability weighting. Promote discipline through training and embedded user assistance.

Automating Quality Checks

Humans make mistakes, so plan for proactive controls ensuring policies stick. Build periodic scripts scanning for common errors like invalid area codes and blank required fields. Set alerts for changes to frozen legacy records which may indicate tampering. If volumes allow, enable statistical tools continuously sampling information with mechanisms to quarantine suspicious entries for review. Isolate rather than delete flagged data until underlying root causes are addressed.

Master Data Management

Leveraging a Master Data Management (MDM) hub to centrally store validated, non-transactional entities like products, suppliers and customers pays dividends. MDM systems act as "single sources of truth" supplying clean information to downstream applications like CRMs. Embed robust reconciliation routines in your CRM to push updates from the MDM, fixing duplications and inconsistencies overnight vs. manual intervention. Where MDM is impractical, appoint dedicated data stewards to govern integrity for each domain.

Ongoing Maintenance

View data health as an iterative process requiring ongoing investment, not a one-time initiative. Build regular data reviews into staff cadences to validate latest inputs and uncover new issues. Keep an eye on adoption levels of validation tools, policy compliance statistics and audit outcomes as lead indicators forecasting emerging gaps to address proactively. Sustain momentum through continuous process improvements addressing root causes for errors.

High-integrity customer and performance data is table stakes for successfully leveraging any CRM. Mitigate risk from the outset through strong governance policies, validation enforcement and automation. Measure and incentivize data excellence at both system and human levels. When information is trustworthy, decisions and actions naturally become smarter.

Harness the Power of CRM Automation

Automation conjures fears of impersonal, robotic customer interactions. However, thoughtfully applied to internal workflows, triggers and alerts, automation acts as a force multiplier realizing immense efficiency gains. The ideal automation delivers impactful yet responsible process use cases to help sales and service professionals work smarter.

Lead Management Activities

CRM platforms shine managing inbound leads through targeted, personalized messaging shaped to individuals' buying stage. Configure intuitive automations like sending key collateral pieces once a visitor crosses an engagement threshold. Build segmented email campaigns nurturing net new, re-engaged and at-risk leads until sales rep assignment. Automatically enroll hand raisers in drip sequences delivering value over time, allowing reps to focus on highest potential opportunities.

Enhancing Sales Productivity

Empower sellers to be more effective by removing manual tasks better handled programmatically. Build templates centralizing commonly referenced material like RFP responses, capability overviews and contract docs to start new deals faster. Trigger notifications to prompt timely customer follow-ups around renewals, escalations and pauses. Prioritize tasks in rep workflows through automated lead scoring and intelligent routing based on keywords and profiles.

Service & Support Optimization

Automating currently high-touch support activities reduces costs while still providing exemplary experiences. Instantly greet new customers with self-help portals and virtual agents handling common inquiries. Escalate complex tickets to reps based on natural language and sentiment analysis vs. after lengthy waits. Keep users informed through status updates as issues progress behind the scenes. Proactively surface knowledgebase articles related to posted questions.

Actionable Analytics & Alerting

While most solutions furnish standard reporting, custom automations transform CRM data into targeted, timely insights democratizing access to intelligence for all. Pipe key monthly metrics into executive dashboards maintaining strategy's pulse. Configure alerts around lead velocity, contract gaps or churn predictors affording early visibility into risks. Tag key accounts requiring closer oversight due to sensitivity. Build weekly data extracts powering complementary analysis tools for power users.

Guardrails & Governance

Automating CRM activities provides undeniable leverage but also risks running on autopilot, misallocating resources. Establish governance upfront through requirements gathering, security protocols and transparent decision logic powering scripts. Pilot changes with control groups before organization-wide rollout. Monitor for unexpected impacts like lowered human touch harming customer satisfaction. Allow easy opt-outs and overrides to inputs. As capabilities advance, reassess automation ethics beyond simple efficiency.

Sustaining Quality at Scale

The most elegant automation loses potency over time absent proper data inputs, maintenance and iteration. Logically organize scripts under ownership of business teams incented to keep functionality current. Schedule periodic reviews assessing whether triggers align to latest processes or require tweaking. Monitor failure rates and user feedback closely to catch issues before business impact. Keep a backlog of enhancement requests prioritized by expected ROI. Tuning and enhancement sustain relevancy amid shifting customer expectations and strategic realignments.

Applied judiciously, CRM automation serves as a strategic accelerator realizing outsized productivity gains while respecting customer experience. Prioritize high-impact activities demonstrated to lift sales, service and analytical performance. Continuously align automated capabilities to evolving operational needs through governance and iterative improvement to maintain competitive differentiation as detailed in Chapter 6.

Build User Competency Continously

Sophisticated CRM platforms mean little without skilled users unlocking capabilities through consistent, thoughtful adoption. Beyond one-time knowledge transfer, leading organizations cultivate enduring competency through layered skill-building addressing different learning styles and evolving needs. Below are several frameworks to train employees for maximum self-sufficiency.

Securing Executive Commitment

Lasting proficiency starts from the top through clear mandates, tone setting and resource allocation. Have business leadership co-develop a multi-year vision for a highly capable staff supplemented by technology. Embed training completion rates into manager scorecards with clear review procedures for non-compliance. Allocate dedicated analysts producing training artifacts and governing materials' relevance as processes shift. Stage recognitions for top completors and internal experts willing to mentor peers.

Multi-Modal Training Formats

Classroom sessions suit foundational concepts but falter addressing varied use cases at scale. Take an omni-channel approach combining eLearning modules, micro-learning videos, quick reference cards, interactive guides, peer discuss boards and gamified skill assessments. This exposes more staff to key learnings through preferred mediums while offering options for reference or reinforcement later. Centralize assets on a community portal also housing analyst contact details and technical documentation.

Role-Based Prioritization

AvoidINFORMATION overload by customizing programs around learners' workflow relevance. Sales staff likely care most about opportunity management, pipeline reporting and proposal generation while service agents need case deflection tools and knowledge base content. Start with must-have areas driving immediate productivity tailoring electives over time or through self-guided discovery. Personalization improves motivation and retention—staff should clearly connect training to real-world application.

Competency Measurement

Quantitatively assess skill uptake early and often, using friendly yet actionable scoring. Embed brief knowledge checks during modules allowing instant feedback on grasping concepts before proceeding. Schedule skills evaluation biannually through simulated workflow exercises scoring speed, accuracy and sophistication unlocking new system functionality. Maintain visibility into adoption through assignment completion rates and self-assessments. Address underperforming areas with targeted coaching and content improvements.

Sustaining Engagement Long-term

Ongoing education sustains hard-earned proficiency against inevitable turnover and platform changes. Encourage peer mentoring through forums recognizing top contributors for assisting struggling users. Incent more advanced workers to create homegrown tips and tricks guides to internalize institutional knowledge. Bring back early training as "refresher editions" with updated examples and new features now relevant to constituents. The strongest learners graduate to co-develop coursework and mentor rising peers over time.

Maximizing intricate CRM investments relies on nurturing sophisticated internal expertise through continuous, tailored learning frameworks elevating individual capability and cultural dexterity. Right-size curricula and assessments to balance functional coverage, prioritizing role relevance over platform familiarity alone.

Make Informed Decisions Through CRM Intelligence

Customer data is rapidly becoming business' most valuable asset. CRMs sit on a goldmine—centralizing critical behavioral, transactional and communication records powering strategic initiatives around revenue growth, retention and operational excellence. Yet insight requires more than aggregation alone. Below are some techniques that help organizations translate raw information into intelligence for competitive advantage.

Embedding Analysis in Processes

Transition teams from sporadic report viewers to continuously data-informed decision makers through systematization. Catalog existing reports, dashboards and models supporting core sales, marketing and service activities. Identify analysis gaps where crucial choices lack factual input. Build templates guiding systematic incorporation of intelligence into planning exercises, investment prioritization and performance reviews. Eliminate data being sought manually by automating routine deliverables like executive briefings, KPI refresh and alert distribution.

Uncovering Behavioral Insights

Looking beyond aggregate performance, explore linking granular activity to outcomes revealing causal relationships between actions and results. Connect lead disposition to historical communications engagement highlighting patterns across converted accounts like video consumption. Review multiple touches preceding sales through Markov chain analysis quantifying effective nurturing sequences. Examine chatter contentpredicting defections based on expressed sentiments. Reveal channel-specific conversion Funnel patterns shaping resource allocation. Behavioral analytics substantially sharpens strategy.

Optimizing Staff Alignment

Cascade metrics alignment through the organization with reporting tailored to each team's impact supporting executives in managing business outcomes. Connect frontline actions to portfolio targets, empowering independent prioritization while maintaining focus on the greater vision. Perfect consistency from corporate goals to individual KRAs using methodology simplifying translations.ServiceData and marketing analysts should see their specific contributions manifesting in chasing critical organization-wide progress markers, driving ownership.

Automating Actions from Alerts

Build workflows triggered by intelligence for rapid response at machine speed otherwise lacking. Configure alerts for rising inquiry backlogs, price ceiling breaches by competitors or high-value customer drop-off indications immediately distributing cases to specialized reps. Instantly enroll VIP contacts meeting criteria predictive of big spending into high-touch nurturing tracks. Drive prospects to targeted content when displaying signals of advanced consideration stages. Allow data to direct real-time priority shifts absent meetings.

External Data Fusion

No single source provides complete coverage; tap outside signals offering orthogonal views to validate hypotheses. Geo-locate leads for firmographic modeling using IP addresses. Incorporate news events and social listening highlighting emerging customer needs. Assimilate economic indicators, regional employment metrics and channel-specific projections to size opportunities. Fuse first-and third-party inputs through correlation to strengthen confidence beyond what internal data alone allows.

Operationalizing Analytical Talent

Insights mean little if unseen by cross-functional leaders driving strategy and execution. Break analytical siloes through embedding roles within business units. Create hybrid contributor tracks rewarding deep functional fluency as highly as technical prowess to bridge gaps. Build analyst rotations into operating rhythms through standing invitations to key meetings, systematizing their voices into planning. Normalize bringing fact-based evidence to discussions by expecting practitioners to furnish supporting materials using self-serve reporting.

Enabling Self-Service Adoption

Place basic analysis directly in users' hands instead of fully intermediating through specialists. Configure dashboards, reports and alerts to be adjusted dynamically on self-service analytics platforms without IT bottlenecks. Automate curated deliverables through scheduled distribution and in-workflow visibility. Implement permissions allowing controlled direct data access rather than solely through rigid reports. Promote utilization through recognitions for contributions and training on analytical soft skills. Democratization drives widespread business ownership.

Continuous System Improvement

Treat intelligence transformation as a journey rather than defined end state amid continually evolving data scale, technology disruption and skill set advances. Develop feedback channels facilitating user submissions of enhancement ideas around reporting gaps, tool deficiencies and emerging use cases. Task a team with keeping pulse on innovations like conversational interfaces, augmented analytics and predictive modeling to interject state-of-art solutions maintaining competitiveness. Keep pace with exponential change.

Leveraging analytics is an imperative rather than a nicety. Embed robust intelligence into workflows company-wide fueled by internal and external data. Arm staff to drive insight-informed decisions through automation, augmentation and democratization. For more information on CRM Reports and Analysis, see Chapter 10.

Improve the Customer Experience Through CRM

CRM technology has long promised transformational connections between brands and individuals. Yet absent thoughtful coordination, disjointed engagements frustrate rather than captivate target audiences. This section outlines strategies to evolve CRMs from tracking systems into centralized experience hubs choreographing unified cross-channel journeys winning satisfied loyalists.

Mapping Current State Flaws

Start by auditing existing pathways through sales, service and marketing lenses exposing cross-functional misalignments impairing experiences. Look for inconsistent messaging as prospects traverse websites then call centers. Identify data gaps preventing continuity between offline and online interactions. Call out redundant contacts aggravating customers. Benchmark current state performance metrics like satisfaction, renewals and referrals to size the opportunity for optimization.

Envisioning Ideal Journeys

With gaps clear, envision optimized routes aligning teams while delighting patrons. Plot lifecycle stage-specific journeys addressing buyers' evolving needs from initial interest cultivation through retention and expansion. Detail required individualized interactions across channels according to historical behaviors and explicit preferences. Specify supporting processes, content and metrics realizing seamless movement. Obtain stakeholder input then executive sign-off cementing cross-departmental commitment towards renovated experiences.

Configuring Unified Platforms

Disjointed technologies themselves disrupt interactions through disjointed datasets and scattered workflows. Standardize on integrated CRM suites consolidating engagement data, analytics, automation and intelligence administration capabilities in one place. Select solutions with robust configuration tools and extensibility to mold around desired pathways rather than settling for generic out-of-box constructs. Customize fields, objects, workflows, sentiment dashboards and predictive recommendation tools realizing differentiated yet coordinated engagements.

Orchestrating Omni-Channel Delivery

Armed with a centralized engagement hub, intentionally align previously siloed activities into unified journeys flawlessly transitioning across channels. Launch online advertisement sequences tailored to recent browsing behaviors auto-enrolling converts into nurture tracks serving complementary content. Make chat windows available straight from personalized landing pages to facilitate real-time question resolution. Hand-off callers to specialized representatives based on sentiment analysis and account scores for contextual, empathetic assistance.

Continuous Optimization

View journey enhancement as an ongoing initiative not a one-time event, building capabilities iteratively while maintaining focus on the North Star vision. Regularly refresh journey maps and orchestration protocols through periodic assessments spotting new friction points as processes and technologies inevitably evolve. Maintain an enhancement idea backlog prioritizing requests via customer impact and effort. Celebrate quick wins maintaining momentum while pursuing long-term milestones advancing sophistication.

Modern consumers demand coordinated cross-channel connections aligning to their needs, not functional silos. CRMs uniquely position organizations to deliver exceptional experiences through data-driven journey orchestration. Center CX initiatives on unified engagement platforms enrolling prospects into lifecycle interactions personalized across sales, service and marketing.

Audit and Update the CRM For Sustained Relevance

Launch represents beginnings not endings for mission-critical CRM investments, which unavoidably drift from optimal configurations over time. Regular health checks and incremental enhancements sustain alignment to shifting operational landscapes across processes, personnel and technologies preventing irrelevance.

Scheduled Assessments

Treat tuning as a standard operating rhythm not an ad-hoc fire drill. Institute quarterly reviews examining recent usage volumes, user feedback surveys, data integrity indicators and performance metrics vis-à-vis targets. Document achieved quick wins, outstanding gaps, upcoming priorities, technological considerations and budget impacts for steering committee input on needed system course corrections. Time insights to feed annual planning and budgeting cycles securing resources proactively.

Updating Taxonomies

Even "locked" elements like customer segments, product catalogs and sales stage probability weightings shift subtly over time warranting periodic adjustments. Keep classifications contemporary and representative through annual taxonomy reviews scrutinizing categorizations against latest behaviors and priorities. Modernize labels matching actual vernacular vs. legacy holdovers causing confusion. Add granularity where maturation supports new cuts on longstanding groupings now masking strategic insights.

Ongoing Data Hygiene

Absent vigilance, data integrity inevitably decays as users overlook standards, gaps go undetected and deficiencies compound. Ensure continuity through policies mandating inclusion of complete customer and opportunity details for updated records. Automate quality checks spotlighting missing elements for follow-up. Centralize reference data governance under data stewards verifying alignment of code tables, valid format patterns, and other structures to current needs. Proactively address root causes behind errors to prevent bad data at the source.

Responding to Emerging Needs

Static systems fail growing organizations. Continuously gather input on desired enhancements through meetings, surveys and monitoring help desk request volumes indicating capability gaps. Stack rank ideas by expected impact and implementation difficulty to prioritize additions like new activity automations, upgraded reporting packages and added integration touchpoints punching above their weight advancing strategic goals. Carve out continuous improvement backlogs even the most mature platforms.

Updating to Latest Functionality

Balance maximizing existing system utility and staying current on new offerings through judicious tech revs every 2-3 years. Major upgrades incorporate valuable step-function innovations like predictive intelligence, enhanced process configurators and emerging channel capabilities securing resiliency against disruptive competition. Take advantage of existing investments by inserting interim dot releases applying version-to-version security patches and minor fixes at more frequent intervals to minimize disruption.

Effective CRMs constantly evolve solving yesterday's problems while anticipating tomorrow's needs. Build iterations into governance routines through
scheduled assessments, continuous enhancements and technology refresh cycles.

Chapter Thirteen

Conclusion: Mastering CRM for Sales Excellence

A cross the preceding chapters, we explored strategies and tactics to elevate sales performance through customer relationship management excellence. When carefully implemented, CRMs serve as true competitive differentiators driving efficiency, intelligence and customer-centricity lifting revenue to new heights. Here, we synthesize key takeaways into a concise framework securing maximum value from CRM investments.

Key Takeaways

Several consistent themes emerged providing a blueprint for sales leaders seeking to realize CRMs' full potential within their organizations:

1. Progress Requires Commitment Beyond Technology

A common misstep organizations make is over-indexing on software sophistication assuming advanced functionality alone will catalyze transformation. However, CRM excellence relies on much more than features, leaning heavily on thoughtful program governance and organizational commitment to value creation. Leaders must reinforce importance through consistent messaging, resource allocation and improvement frameworks securing solution relevance over years.

Begin by securing executive sponsorship early, tying technology priorities into strategic growth plans winning leadership buy-in. Engage deeply with user groups in solution evaluations determining pain points, ideal workflows and reporting needs that chosen platforms absolutely must address even potentially at the expense of other functions. This focus on organizational fit ensures relevance over chasing bells and whistles alone.

Once live, stay perpetually opportunistic expanding utility through continuous enhancement better serving customers and operations. Maintain backlogs prioritizing future functionality improvements through regular listening touchpoints welcoming ideas companywide. Enact data governance policies and training upholding information integrity as utilization scales over time.

Progress requires organizational diligence not just vendor version releases.

2. Alignment to Strategy Comes First

Misaligned platforms fail realizing intended outcomes regardless of technical capability. Always start any CRM initiative by tightly defining business objectives, end-user requirements and success metrics to guide software selection and configuration ensuring deep alignment to revenue goals from the outset. Importing disjointed data or workflows reflecting longstanding broken processes only exacerbates existing issues. Leadership must set the tone for CRM priorities before launch.

Assemble implementation teams encompassing varied perspectives including departmental heads, frontline personnel, analytics experts and technical specialists weighing needs holistically. Conduct detailed opportunity analyses quantifying revenue expansion, customer experience and productivity lift realizable through rationalized data-driven engagements, arming leadership with tangible targets. Once live, connect platform analytics directly into planning processes and performance reviews cementing centrality to sales strategy.

Carefully script demonstrative business use cases applied systematically against vendors reflecting realistic utilization patterns and data volumes, stress testing application stability with an eye toward sustainable long-term architecture. Allow intended users hands-on trial participation to confirm functional fit beyond paper checklists, facilitating buy-in. Rigorous evaluations followed by participative rollout instill strategy alignment from the start.

3. Value Creation Should Be Measurable

CRM projects universally rely on expected performance lift justifying investments, yet rarely establish credible measurement frameworks validating technology value post-implementation. By mandating consistent tracking of process improvements' business impact, leadership both maintains outcome focus during rollout and produces irrefutable ROI proofs for future budget requests. Make contribution traces non-negotiable.

Enact success tracking processes with regular operational and financial reviews quantifying platform influence on advancing top-line performance metrics demonstrating credible system value. Estimate sales velocity, customer retention and servicing cost improvements by triangulating historical data with other process changes and expert estimates when perfect isolation proves difficult. Continuously communicate broad revenue and managerial productivity wins securing goodwill easing additional initiatives' approval down the road.

Require proposal owners to forecast returns ahead of funding commitment through detailed models reflecting return timeframes, budget impacts and productivity gains. An initiative promising to save 1,000 CSR hours annually through script elimination is praiseworthy but lacks context; estimating $50,000 annual savings from 20% increased response throughput provides compelling motivation. Tracking both output and outcome-based key performance indicators creates accountability for producing real business results not just technology implementation alone.

4. Adoption is Best Promoted Through Enablement

Sophisticated platforms mean little absent thoughtful adoption strategies addressing people, process and skills-building. CRM success relies on users' willingness and ability to leverage capabilities advancing individual and organizational goals. Beyond one-time knowledge transfer, leading organizations invest in layered skill-building addressing different learning styles and evolving sophistication needs cementing sticky usage.

Support stakeholders through multi-modal training suites including classroom workshops, micro-learning videos, quick reference cards, peer discusses and gamified assessments tailored to various groups' interests and workflows. Customize modules to roles, optimizing time through emphasis on must-have areas driving everyday productivity. Maintain always-available online support portals centralized with expert contacts, technical documentation and discussion forums sustaining proficiency post-training.

Enable power users by connecting platform analytics into planning processes and performance reviews, cementing centrality to sales operations. Build regular platform reviews into cadences tracking adoption levels, enhancing feature relevance to current processes. Institute friendly usage competitions and skills certifications incentivizing engagement. Through continuous learning and governance frameworks, organizations transform passive system users into truly proficient power players achieving CRM mastery.

5. Optimization Never Stops as Needs Evolve

Static solutions fail growing organizations. Markets move quickly - what suffices today likely will not cutting-edge tomorrow. Maintain sharpness by treating deployments as platforms ripe for continuous enhancement through both technological improvements and process innovations. Stay opportunistic expanding utility even for mature implementations.

Task CRM owners with quarterly reviews tuning offerings' alignment to evolving operational needs and market offerings, maintained through standing listening cycles, enhancement backlogs and benchmarking. Actively gather inputs on desired upgrades through meetings, surveys monitoring help desk request volumes indicating adoption gaps or emerging feature wish lists. Stack rank ideas by expected impact and implementation difficulty, carving out continuous improvement capacity securing relevance.

Make technology revitalization a standard 3-year project synchronizing with budgeting cycles, balancing migration costs against innovations in intelligence, workflow and user experiences. Major upgrades incorporate valuable step-function innovations like predictive analytics, customized process configurators and emerging channel capabilities securing resiliency against disruptive competition. Take advantage of existing investments by inserting interim dot releases applying minor fixes between versions minimizing disruption.

By perpetually enhancing effectiveness through both technological improvements and process innovations, organizations sustain differentiation enjoying outsized customer relationship management returns for years atop careful foundations ensuring strategy alignment, measurable outcomes and broad enablement from the start.

Constructing Continuous Improvement Plans

Yet mastery develops through structured expansion of capability over time, not overnight wins. Sales heads should codify ONGOING enhancement frameworks ensuring solutions adapt to ever-changing sales landscapes:

- Mandate quarterly feature assessment identifying emerging use cases to tackle through configurations or procured apps

- Enact annual technology reviews balancing migration costs against innovations in AI, workflow and UX

- Maintain an enhancement backlog stacked by ROI continuously refined through idea inputs

- Task CRM ownership teams with capability benchmarking against peers highlighting new learnings for internal adoption

- Develop feedback channels surveying users on strengths, gaps and wish lists

- Report on usage rates by team and feature area guiding education investment

Relentlessly Growing CRM Acumen

But technology is only half the equation - realizing full CRM potential requires nurturing sophisticated internal expertise through continuous, tailored learning frameworks elevating individual capability and cultural dexterity:

- Secure executive commitment around skills development through mandates and funding

- Curate role-based learning paths aligning to salesperson needs from modules to mentoring

- Measure adoption through usage, proficiency assessments and certifications

- Incentive ongoing education through recognitions, awards and growth opportunities

- Sustain proficiency through peer mentoring and new hire training programs

By pairing purposeful technological improvement with ambitious organizational capability building, sales chiefs can unleash CRM's full promise revolutionizing sales engagement, productivity and profitability over the long term.

The sales leaders who will win tomorrow are those establishing customer-centric foundations today. CRM excellence relies on much more than software capabilities alone, leaning heavily on thoughtful program governance and commitment to value creation. By investing in robust functional evaluations, customer-centric rollout strategies and value tracking processes, sales executives can secure solution relevance over years achieving differentiated relationship management maturity setting their customer engagement leagues ahead of peers still struggling with deployment basics. The frameworks and philosophies detailed here chart that course to mastery.

www.ingramcontent.com/pod-product-compliance
Lightning Source LLC
Chambersburg PA
CBHW072201290526
45794CB00004B/1603